"We write the history today for the children of tomor̶̶̶̶̶"

After an evening of Music and Heritage which took place at the ̶̶̶̶̶̶ to Raharney Church) last July, 2022 we were reminded to pass o̶̶̶̶̶ of knowledge about our townlands, about our people and abou̶̶̶̶ documents. We then decided to come together to write this book.

Shay Callaghan, with an in-depth interest in history, has provided us with an enriched understanding of life in Raharney down through the years. He eloquently recalls 'Tommy the Shoemaker' and 'Tom Ivory, the Blacksmith' 'Grangemore House' to mention but a few, drawing us into the physical, emotional and geographical landscape of the place where he grew up.

Shay Murtagh (our patron) has a treasure trove of information about his business, his relatives and their work patterns, not forgetting vibrant memories of being in Spike Island.

Rita Monaghan has stepped back in time with records of the shareholders of Thomastown Mill in Killucan, a townland close to her heart. Her written account of Matt Gartland is pure history at its best.

Anne Maher travels with unvarnished clarity to Clonycavan Bog, the Congo and Chernobyl. She includes a few poems into the bargain.

Lillie Connaughton steps back in time with a display of remarkable photographs, gathered from bottom drawers and old leather-bound photo albums. Such a daunting task! She was in charge of the Wedding Section, so whether by accident or design it goes to show that romance is still very much alive in Raharney.

Annette Farrell has taken a more complex approach. She looked after the Religious side of things including Kilcolumb Cemetery and the Raharney Gun Club, assuring us that there is no real connection, other than a literary one!

What comes into sharp focus is how the 5th and 6th Class Raharney schoolchildren have enriched us so much with their enthusiastic essays and research. Their distinctive voices will no doubt fascinate our readers.
This gem of a collection contains some of the most original collection of stories ever, and will most definitely add to our conversations in Raharney and across the globe.

Our thanks to the sponsors of the school prizes and to all who have helped us along the way, Joe Mullen who listened to our woes and Mary Dunne who was willing to type our stories at the drop of a hat. Lastly, a heart-felt thanks to Aisling and Colm Kerr of Arc Studios, Raharney, for all their profound support and hard work, particularly for their belief in the healing power of stories and photographs.

Thank you!
Anne Maher

ST BRIDGETS CHURCH
RAHARNEY
A HISTORY

1750

THERE IS SOME DEBATE ABOUT WHERE IN THE VILLAGE THE FIRST CHURCH WAS SITUATED IN RAHARNEY. ANECDOTAL EVIDENCE SAYS IT WAS SITUATED CLOSE TO THE SIDE AND REAR OF THE LATE PHYLLIS WHITES HOUSE, AND BUILT AROUND THE YEAR 1750. IT HAD A THATCHED ROOF; TWO STONE CROSSES AT THE BACK OF THE PRESENT CHURCH ARE SAID TO BE FROM THAT CHURCH. IT IS ALSO SAID THAT AFTER THE PRESENT CHURCH WAS BUILT, FARMERS WERE ALLOWED TO TRASH THEIR CORN IN THE OLD CHURCH WITH FLAILS BECAUSE OF THE HIGH CEILING, PROVIDED THEY LEFT STRAW FOR THATCHING.IT IS BELIEVED THE FARMERS BROUGHT THEIR CORN ACROSS THE RIVER TO THE HILL BESIDE THE MILL, VIA A FORD BESIDE THE DAM, TO REMOVE THE CHAFF

1834

The present St Bridget's Church was built in 1834 by Father Curren.P.P. A lease in the diocesan archives dated 4th March 1834 grants to Fr Curran "all that are part of the lands of Rathfarne in the possession of James White containing thirty perches for the purpose of erecting a Roman Catholic Church theron"

1860

The Church was renovated in 1860 by Father Eugene O'Rourke and dedicated to St Bridget. Funds for this work were raised locally and the U.S.A. by emigrants from the parish.

1900

A holy water font inside the long aisle door was donated by Christopher Murray in memory of his family who also emigrated from Raharney to New York

1903

William Alphonsus Scott a well known architect from Drogheda, updated and renovated the church.

1905

The 3 stained-glass windows at the back of the altar were sponsored by a group of emigrants from Raharney called the "Raharney Rovers" in New York.

Entertainment and Reception
OF THE
Raharney Rover
Social Club
At Mr. M. J. JENNINGS' HALL
69th Street and Third Ave.
Friday, March 17th, 1905
ST. PATRICK'S NIGHT
Music by Prof. Fitzpatrick Champion Irish Piper and Full Orchestra
Souvenir Ticket of Raharney Chapel County Westmeath, Ireland. 25 Cents
Proceeds of Entertainment to be used in completing Repairs on Raharney Chapel

1965+

As a result of Vatican II, the Church made changes to its mass, allowing the liturgy to be translated to the vernacular and allowing the priest to face the congregation. Changes now needed to be made to the layout of the altar. It was hoped these changes would encourage the participation of the laity.
At this time there was a passageway behind the altar from one vestry to the other. The altar was moved back against the gable wall and was re-constructed into its present position. The altar rails were also removed.

1988

In 1988 major renovations were carried out. The architects were Messrs. Smith and Kennedy, Dublin and the main contractor was local ,man Mr P.J. Keogh. The work included the erection of three new porches, newly designed sanctuary, new windows and doors, new boiler and boiler house, re wiring, new floor and seats, interior and exterior painting and landscaping of the grounds. It was rededicated by Most Rev. Michael Smith on Sunday October nd, 1988.

2022

In recent times a new building has been constructed beside the church, with outstanding facilities, including new technology whereby parishioners all over the world can view all church services online. All this has been sponsored solely by Shay Murtagh in a new building that was once Ciss and Josie Holdrights house and small shop.

(Top left) 1932 - The holy water font inside the long aisle door was donated by Christopher Murray in memory of his family who emigrated from Raharney to New York *(Top right)* The altar in 1963 and today *(Bottom left)* L-R Back: Mary Harris, Lil Hickey, Mick Swords, Mary (Babs) Price, Mary Flanagan, Vera Mulvany, Maureen Donoghue, Lil Connor, L-R Front: Nea & Mulvany Children *(Bottom reight)* Our Lady's Grotto - The Rosary has always been recited during the month of May at Our Lady's Grotto. [Image: Arc Studios]

Our Lady's Grotto

The stone plaque in front of the Grotto reads "Our Lady's Grotto, opened and blessed by Most Rev. Dr. McCormack, Bishop of Meath, Sunday 22 June 1969." Tommy Reilly (Post Office), Frank Murtagh, Joe Doyle (senior), Joe Mooney, Seamus Brennan (School Master) Peter Mulkerins, Peter Davitt, John McKenna, and Tom Riggs organized the cleaning up of the Grotto and removing the pile of briars which had taken over the spot. Master Brennan organised the schoolchildren to pull weeds after school, an hour each evening with permission from their parents.

Kilcolumb Church & Cemetery

Kilcolumb. Cill (Kill) Church, probably with association to Columb. Gravestones indicate that burials took place on a raised site above the River Deel after 1700. The ruins of a small stone church suggest that there was a previous use of the site. The possibility that St. Columcille (Columba) born in Garten, Donegal and a student of St. Finian of Clonard Monastery which housed 3,000 students at one time may have visited the site giving rise to suggestion of an association with perhaps a monk living on this site who he may have called to on his way home from Clonard to Kells, the monastery which Colmcille founded as well as his other famous abbeys at Derry, Durrow, and Swords.

Reference: O' Conluain R.M.P. W.M. P02d1-00809 Kilcolumb listed under Grangebeg, Co. Westmeath. No. 94 in Study.

[Image: Arc Studios]

Graveyard Project:

The irregular shape of the graveyard hints at a very early date 1700-1760. There are a variety of cut-stone markers dating from 1700-1920. The ruins of a single-story chapel on rectangular base to the centre. This has collapsed.

In the cemetery there is a collection of upstanding and recumbent markers from early 18th century, one with fine craftmanship. The date of the church is not discernible but small size and rough form suggest pre-1700. Fr. Patrick Sherlock and his predecessor Rev. Fr. John Swords, a native of Rathrass, (where the Swords family still live) died in 1821 and said Masses in the old Church Raharney. They are both interred in Kilcolumb. Many cures were attributed to Fr. Sword's during the mid 1800's when emigration to America was at its peak. It was the practice of emigrants to take a small portion of clay from his grave with them on their journey.

In a small area walled off from the main graveyard is the burial plot of the Briscoes. They were the principal property owners in the area and owned the land where Kilcolumb Graveyard is situated. Kilcolumb Graveyard, Raharney and Knockmant Graveyard on the Mullingar Road are both built on a hill surrounded by a wall.

I.G.P. Westmeath Genealogy Archives Records:

There is a list of the names of people interred in Kilcolumb Cemetery compiled by Alan Murphy and aided by Sean Swords. This includes the names of over seventy families listed.

A meeting was held on Tuesday, 29th June 2010 in St. Brigid's Church, Raharney regarding the restoration of Kilcolumb Graveyard. A large crowd attended the meeting. Fr. Richard Matthews P.P. spoke about the wishes of the people of Raharney and himself to have Kilcolumb Graveyard restored and cleaned up, so that the people can visit and pay their respects to those buried there. Apologies were sent from a number of those who could not attend the meeting but submitted their names and telephone numbers for future meetings.

Fr. Matthews called on Eddie Deihy to speak. Eddie, who was on the committee for Knockmant Graveyard, on the Mullingar Road, Killucan, detailed how they went about applying for a grant to do up the graveyard. He explained the various stages of the clean-up and how the work was carried out. Shay Murtagh told how he contacted the owner of the land who kindly gave permission for a road being made, leading up to the graveyard. It was also decided to have photographs taken of the headstones in the graveyard before the clean-up began, and through the various stages of the work being carried out, Noel Greville agreed to take on this job. Jim Farrelly agreed to take on the job as supervisor and with his knowledge he will be a great asset to the project.

Another topic discussed – that the people themselves would come forward with information, names, dates, etc. of relatives or neighbours buried here. Nominations were then received for the election of officers. They are as follows:

Chairperson: Sean Swords, **Secretary:** Geraldine McManus, **Treasurer:** Ursula Swords, **Supervisor:** Jim Farrelly, **Photographer:** Noel Greville, **Committee:** Jim Farrelly, Chris Farrelly, Joseph Mullen, Jonny McKeogh, Sean Swords, Sean McKenna, Gerry Quinn, Gerry O'Connor, Shay Murtagh, M. Jennett, Sean Coyne, Sinead Nea, Teresa Nea, Sean Nea, Nicholas Weir, M. Boyle, Paddy Mulvaney, Aine Holdwright, Seamus Holdwright, Brendan Farrelly, Nonnie Farrelly, Kitty Mulvaney, Mollie Doyle, Paul O'Looney, Valerie McHugh, Margo Farrelly Fitzsimons, Geraldine McManus, Helen Doyle, Michael Doyle, Ursula Swords, Edward Foxe, Tom Bray, Noel Greville, Tommy O'Connor and Tom O'Rourke. *29th June 2010*

A full list of those buried in this graveyard can be viewed at
https://www.igp-web.com/IGPArchives/ire/westmeath/cemeteries/kilcolumb.html

Note: We are aware that many other souls may be buried in this graveyard and are not named. There is an Easter Sunday Dawn Mass at 6am in Kilcolumb Cemetery annually. The last burial in Kilcolumb Cemetery was that of Patrick Davitt 31st December 1989 the coffin had to be carried in through the field.

School in Raharney

Angela Farrelly

Angela Farrelly is the current Principal of Raharney NS. She was appointed in 1993 following the retirement of her father. It was not a job she had envisaged in her path, but life works in mysterious ways.

A native of Raharney she attended Raharney National School. She inherited her father's love of music and played the accordion in the school band for many years. The Church choir was an inherent part of their family history, and her memories include singing at three Masses on Christmas morning. When the organist died, she sourced an electric organ that played tracks enabling the choir to keep going for many years.

Her passion was and is sport. Following her dad around from an early age fostered her love for hurling and camogie. She played underage and Senior for Raharney Camogie Club with many long and hard matches being fought against St. Munna's, their strongest opponents at that time. In 1981 Angela Farrell was awarded 'Camogie Player' of the year by Westmeath GAA. She continued to play club and county camogie until the early '90's. Angela then switched to training and spent several years training the Senior Raharney camogie team.

Her love for sports continues in the school where she encourages the pupils to play GAA games and trains them for Cumann na mBunscol.

Angela Farrelly.

Angela's Secondary school days were spent in Loreto College, Mullingar. She represented Loreto in hockey and tennis competitions. Her aim was always to be a teacher and she continued to St. Patrick's College, Drumcondra. Once qualified she spent her first few years teaching in St. Joseph's, Rathwire and Loughegar School. In 1990 she was appointed as a permanent teacher in Raharney National School.

In 1990 she married Michael Farrelly, and they have 3 children. As a family they all became involved in Badminton. Winning a Leinster and then an All-Ireland Badminton medal on a Westmeath team with her 2 sons is a precious achievement.

Seamus Brennan - The Village School Master

Seamus Brennan first came to Raharney at the age of 24, when he was appointed Principal of Raharney National School. He was not a total stranger to this part of the country as he was born in Ballivor where his father was stationed as a guard. At the age of 7 his father was transferred to Mullingar Garda Station and 8 Harbour Street became his home. His primary education was received in St. Mary's C.B.S. He was awarded a scholarship to continue his education at Coláiste Einde, Co.

[Image: Arc Studios]

Galway and Ballyvourney, Co. Cork. He wanted to become a teacher and he completed his education in St. Patrick's College, Drumcondra. After graduating he spent four years teaching in Dublin and during this time, he met his future wife, Annie McGettrick. They were married in Dublin in 1952. When they moved to Raharney their first house was a small cottage in Bellview, then they moved to Curristown and finally to the house Seamus renovated in Grangebeg. He and his wife Ann had seven children with their first child dying at birth in Sligo hospital.

His appointment was to the 'old school' that was situated on the Wardenstown Road, but he was very happy when the new school was opened in 1961 and they moved to the centre of Raharney. His enthusiasm for his job was evident over the years as he taught a very wide curriculum. He was a very practical teacher who enjoyed spending time in the garden, doing fretwork and woodwork and playing hurling on the school field.

Seamus Brennan was an avid GAA enthusiast which he claims predominantly came from the many summers spent with his grandmother, who was a midwife in Castletown Geoghegan. His schooling in Cork led to his friendship with Michael Ó Muircheartaigh and other GAA enthusiasts with whom he had many reunions over the years. He brought his love of hurling to Raharney and spent generation after generation nurturing a love of hurling in his pupils. Over many years Seamus played an integral part in Raharney Hurling Club. He fulfilled many roles within the club, such as being instrumental with Tommy McKeogh in putting structures in place for underage teams in 1970's & 1980's, being involved with the first ever Raharney Hurling Team to travel to the National Feile finals in Waterford, being one of the original Trustees for Joristown Park and eventually becoming a lifelong Club President.

Over the years he got involved in many projects and activities in the village. He and Noel Weir secured a field from the Land Commission and then used the trees growing along the side to pay for and develop the land. This field was names 'Joristown Park.' He was also involved in the development and building of the Grotto, the building of the tennis court and pavilion, the three counties league tennis competition, Community games and the Tidy Towns.

Music was another great love of Seamus Brennan with his violin being his favourite instrument to play. He composed many a song for winning occasions and he spent every Sunday on the church gallery co-ordinating the choir with the organist Mary Harris. He brought this love of music into the school with many a young Raharney pupil having their first introduction to learning and playing music under his guidance. He founded a School Band which provided music at enormous parades and special occasions. The band played for the Taoiseach, Albert Reynolds in 1992 when he visited Raharney. He also led the teams unto Cusack Park at the midland Feile in 1984. Memories of sitting on a trailer or walking to Joristown as a member of the band is a strong memory for later pupils of the school.

Seamus Brennan joined the FCA as a young man and thoroughly enjoyed his weekly trip to Columb Army Barracks in Mullingar. As soon as he got his summer holidays from school, he was off to the Glen of Imall, Wicklow for training and shooting practice. He worked his way through the ranks and was very proud when he earned the rank of Commandant.

On Friday 25th June 1993, at the age of 65, Seamus Brennan retired from Raharney National School after more than forty-one years as Principal. It was a job that he had dedicated his life to and he was always very appreciative of the fantastic staff that worked with him in the school over the years. A function was held in Rathwire Hall on the 26th of June to mark his retirement. He also retired from the FCA.

Thus began a new chapter in his life – Life at a much slower pace. He spent most of his time at home with his wife Ann. He invested his time in his garden and spent hours in his glasshouse. He went on holidays with his daughters and their families. He spent time with his grandchildren. Unfortunately, at this stage his wife Ann was starting to develop 'Dementia.' The roles in the house reversed and Seamus took over the everyday duties. One of his proudest moments was when he was nominated for 'Carer of the Year.' He continued to care for Ann until the day he died.

Seamus Brennan passed away on 27th May 2019.

© Angela Farrelly

Year 1926

Raharney Girls Classes, 1926. 1st row, left to right: E. Dargan, Annie Keeffe, Alice Fullam, Massie Dargan, Lil Darcy, Annie Dargan. 2nd row: M. B. Lynch, Agnes Flynn, Mary Keeffe, Margaret Anderson, Girl Unknown, Annie Anderson, Annie Doyle, Tess Fulham, Lil O'Connor, Mollie Flanagan. 3rd row: Nell Corcoran, Bridget Foley, Brigid Dargan, Nancy Corcoran, Ann Farrelly, M. Smyth, E. Conway, Mary Flanagan, Annie Grimes, Girl Unknown, Sheila White, N. J. Grimes, May Lynch, D. Doyle, Nell Flynn. 4th row: E. Conway, M. Flynn, Vera Lynch, Rose Anderson Annie Dargan, M. E. Keoghan, next unknown, Josie Jennett, next unknown, Annie Greville, May Dargan, Nell Flynn, next unknown, Rose Jennett, Kitty Flanagan, Peg Flanagan, K. Duffy, Florie Byrne, Annie Anderson, Lil Dargan. Small boy in photo : Michael Grimes.

1st row, left to right: P. Lynch, J. Fay, H. Fulham, H. Greene, V. Fitzpatrick, T. Farrelly, P. Conway, P. Doyle (the grey), J. Raleigh, J. Mullen. 2nd row: P. Fallon, W. J. Lynch, B. Grimes, P. Flanagan, J. Doyle (Shouk), J. Reilly, G. Foley, B. McGander, C. Cunningham, B. Carney, E. Lynch, B. Flanagan, J. Conway, B. Lynch, S. Corcoran, J. Anderson, P. Connoor. A. Lynch. 3rd row: J. Murtagh, P. McKeogh, M. Whelehan, K. Conway, M. Flynn, Mick Whelehan, L. Byrne, D. Kenny, F. Conway, F. Whelehan, B. Fay. 4th row: J. Anderson, N. Duffy, J. Raleigh, P. Price, B. Murtagh, H. Flanagan, D. Raleigh, A. Lynch, J. McKeogh.

Year 1927

Raharney National School. Left from back row, Maggie Doyle, Tess Fulham, N. Doyle, M. Kilduff, M. Flanagan, M. Dargan, N. Anderson, M.B. Lynch, L. White, L. Darcy, Alice Fulham, N. Keeffe, N. Grimes, M. Anderson, R. Smith, P. Flanagan, N. Corcoran, C. Doolan, Mary Flanagan, Eileen Flanagan, S. White, N. Duffy, B. Foley, R. Anderson, Nell Flynn, N. Greville, F. Byrne, M. Flynn, — Smith, Eithne Conway, K. Duffy and V. Lynch.

Year 1944

Pat Jennette, Patsy Dowdall, Kit Greville, Paddy Lynch, Mick Bray, Sean Dargan, Kit Connolly

Mick Jennette, ? , Jimmy Fulham, Joe Mooney, Jimmy Farrelly, Sean Kane, Jimmy Jennette, Michael 'Rinty' Murray

Where Are They Now?

This photograph of the Junior boys section was taken in front of Raharney Old School 19456/46. Front row, left to right: Jimmy Weir, Wardenstown; Sean Quinn, Joristown; Pat Croash, The Brockas; Mickey Kelly, Inan; Brendan Dargan, Ballinahee; Nickey Weir, Wardenstown; Anthony Weir, Wardenstown; Tommy O'Keeffe, Corbetstown; Michéal Swords, Raharney; Shay Callaghan, Craddenstown. Middle row: Frank Farrell, Clonbore; Maurice Doyle, Ballinahee; Seazmus Holdwright, Brutonstown; Kevin Lynch, Craddenstown; Kit Murtagh, Ballivor; Frank Lynam, Bellview; Matt Mullen, Bellview; Georgie Robinson, Bellview; Joe Shaw, Cloghanstown; Tom Bray, Ballinahee; Séan Swords, Raharney. Back row: Mickey Cannon, Rodney's Hill; Eamon Hickey, Riversdale; Leo Sheils, The Brockas; Michael McKeogh, The Brockas; Tommy Croash, The Brockas; Anthony Mulvaney, Riversdale. It is quite amazing that, while the Forties and Fifties were infamous for the great number of school leavers who emigrated, all but five of the above are presently resident in Ireland and the majority of those within the Parish of Killucan. Those residing abroad are: George Robinson, Mickey Kelly, Frank Lynam and Anthony Mulvaney, England; and Brendan Dargan, Australia. Some of "Townlands" used in the addresses may not be familiar to all nowadays but they are local placenames and were very much in use in those times.

Raharney School Essays

The Raharney History Group decided to host a Writing Competition in the local school asking fifth and sixth class to participate in writing an essay on 'Raharney' and in order to reward them with a sense of gratification and fulfilment the Group felt that the winning essays could be then published in our forthcoming History Book. Angela Farrelly the School Principal, and Mr. Brian Maguire assured us that the class set about this task very enthusiastically looking up information, immediately attempting to accomplish this goal for the required deadline. The First Prize of 100 Euro probably sparked a little something inside of them, not to mention the Second Prize of 50 Euro and Third Prize of 50 euro. The submission criteria was that the essay could be in words, a poem, a drawing/painting or including all three forms.

The standard was excellent, and the History Group would like to commend the 5th and 6th class pupils of Raharney National School on all the hard work they put into their entries. Furthermore, we would like to show our appreciation to the parents, the grannies and grandads, teachers and specially to Mr. Brian Maguire who encouraged the young students to take part. For the children who were not successful this time, we ask that they please continue writing regardless. We are very proud of all the students. A special thanks to the sponsors for their generosity, Fitzsimons Landscaping Contractors, and Weir's Shop, Raharney, and also those who wish to remain anonymous. May success and prosperity follow them and always keep them in Raharney!

© Anne Maher

[Image: Arc Studios]

1st Prize (€100):
Sean
Connell
6th Class

2nd Prize (€50):
Meadhbh
Connaughton Quinn
5h Class

3rd Prize (€50):
Aaron
Mulvaney
6th Class

Honorary Prize (€20):
Dermot
Kavanagh
6th Class

Honorary Prize (€20):
Oisin
Goonery
6th Class

Sean Connell:

St. Mary's N.S., Raharney
Tel: 044 9374310
Email: reception@raharneyns.ie
Website: www.raharneyns.ie

My Raharney Project.

For my Raharney project I asked my Granny who is from Craddenstown Raharney to tell me all about Raharney. My Granny's parents and their parents were all from Raharney.

She showed me some papers that she had from her father, who had kept them from his Father.

This is a 'poor rate' collectors demand note from 1899. This belonged to my Great Great Grandfather Patrick Grogan. The poor rate was a tax that everyone in Ireland had to pay based on how much land or money they had. There was severe poverty in Ireland. This money was collected to pay for the poor houses and workhouses that poor people were forced to go into.

This is a receipt for rent from 1920 when my Great Great Grandfather rented more land. He paid 5 shillings for half a year. In today's money that would have been around €100. He paid it to the Earl of Longford who would have owned most of the land in Raharney and all-around Westmeath. Everyone would have paid him rent.

My granny told me that Raharney was a much bigger village when she was a child in the 1950's. She cycled from Craddenstown into Raharney to school every day. Raharney had a cobbler, which was in the house inside the grand gates (where Tom who goes to this school lives now). There was a baker (in Mrs Farrelly's home house). The house beside Declan's shop was a tailor. There was a butcher in the house across from McHughs. There were 5 shops and 2 pubs. There was a mill race on the Deel just beside the grotto.

Everyone who lived in Raharney worked here or nearby, farming the land or in the bog. There would have been no need to travel into Mullingar very much. People didn't have cars anyway. It was a very different place then. I enjoyed my Granny telling me all about Raharney 100 years ago.

This is a requisition for land certification from 1905 when my Great Great Grandfather bought the land on which he built the house that my Great Grandfather, and my Grandmother were born. He bought 12 acres for £53. The house he built was a very small cottage with two rooms, and a loft. It had no running water, no electricity, no bathroom. It was like this until the 1990's when my uncle got electricity. Craddenstown is in the bog. At the time when he built the house there were lots of houses there and even a shop (in the house where Ms Jordan's parents live, it was called 'Endwood' house.) The shop was there until the 1930's. She told me that there were two hedge schools in Craddenstown. My Great Great Grandfather went to one of these hedge schools.

Meadhbh Connaughton Quinn:

St. Mary's N.S., Raharney
Tel: 044 9374310
Email: reception@raharneyns.ie
Website: www.raharneyns.ie

RAHARNEY

River Deel

Raharney is a little village just outside of Mullingar. Raharney is very passionate about Hurling and Camogie. The village of Raharney has a bridge over the River Deel and is the last settlement of the county on the edge of the bogland that separates Westmeath from County Meath. The bridge links the roads that run North-South alongside the River Deel. The River Deel is a tributary of the Boyne. The roads into the village all slope down towards the river, suggesting that before the bridge was built there was a fjord at this point. Looking westward to Mullingar the village is located in a gap between three large lakes.

Shops

In Raharney there used to be a butchers, post office, shop and a clinic. The old shop was destroyed by a fire in 1963. After that it was rebuilt and renamed Weirs.

Raharney Utd

Raharney United was established in 2003 with the aim to provide coaching and facilities for the community within the Killucan Raharney area. For the 2018/2019 season there were approximately 145 playing members of the club.

Grangemore House

Grangemore House has important historical connections with the Briscoe and later the Fertherston-Haugh family.

School

In 1961 there were just over one hundred pupils in the school. It is noted that the national school was originally to the south of the village

Fairy Forts

There are a couple of fairy forts in Raharney. Some of them are along the banks of the river Deel. It is said that it is bad luck to play hurling/camogie or football in one of the fields in which these forts are because one of the players always gets hurt. In Keeffe's field, Corbetstown there is a fort with a hole in the top but no one has explored the interior. Some people say that churning is done on a fort in Fagan's farm and that the sound can be plainly heard. Music is also said to be heard from the same fort. Raharney has taken its name from" Rath Airne" meaning fort of the sloes. The Deel is crossed in the village by a bridge of five arches that was renovated under a famine relief scheme in 1848. The village is located close to an old burial ground called Kilcolm with a ruined church that was at one time a chapel of ease for Killucan Abbey and afterwards for St Margaret's of Rathwire.

POEM

Raharney is where I call home

Always a friendly face to be seen

Hurling and Camogie Champions

Always bright with Blue and White

River Deel flowing strong

National School at the heart of the village

Even the Fairies want to live here

You are always welcome in Raharney.

Aaron Mulvaney:

St. Mary's N.S., Raharney
Tel: 044 9374310
Email: reception@raharneyns.ie
Website: www.raharneyns.ie

"FACTS ABOUT RAHARNEY"

Raharney {Ráth Fhearna} Meaning 'Fearna's Ringfort. It is in the parish of Killucan. The village of Raharney has a bridge over the river Deel.

At the back of Weir's shop in Raharney there is an old famine shed. It is still there today under the bridge. It was used for pigs too. In the famine there were some houses in Pudden Lane, that was actually called back then {Pudden Row} but they aren't there anymore. In Raharney there are six roads that lead to different places.

"St Brigid's Church Raharney"

Raharney church used to be near the river. Built in 1834, it is 188 years old today. Grangemore house was built in 1811. Kilcolumb cemetery known as the old graveyard, has headstones dating back to the 18th century.

Where the old petrol pumps are there used to be a post office that a man called Tommy Reilly used to run. There was also a little shop right beside the church that a lady called Mrs Nees owned. We also used to have a shop across from the church called McKeogh's shop.

There are Raharney hurling & camogie clubs. Also Raharney Utd football team. Raharney NS was not always where it is today. The school used to be up the back road just by Village Close estate. My grandad went to that school. Then in the 60's the school we are all standing in today was built.

The Grotto in Raharney, was opened and blessed in 1969. Today, Joe Mullen looks after it making sure it's kept nice and clean.

Thank you for reading my facts about Raharney. I hope you enjoyed the lesson.

Dermot Kavanagh:

St. Mary's N.S., Raharney
Tel: 044 9374310
Email: reception@raharneyns.ie
Website: www.raharneyns.ie

Raharney Story

Raharney is a village in the east of Co. Westmeath in Ireland. It had a population of 221 in the 2016 census.

Raharney is built on the River Deel. The Deel is 22 miles long. It starts from Lough Lene and Lough Bane. It flows into the River Boyne. It is a good river for fishing Brown Trout.

St Marys NS, Raharney was built in **1960** by the Maguire Brothers from Athboy, County Meath. There were extensions built on in 1978 and 2007. There are 87 pupils in the school at the moment. Two members of the band, The Academic went to school in Raharney.

St. Bridget's Church was built in 1834. The Parish Priest is Fr. Stan Deegan.

Raharney Hurling Club is based in Joristown Park on the Killucan Road. There is a strong tradition of hurling and camogie in the village and the teams have been successful at all age levels.

Raharney United is a soccer club based in Higginstown outside Raharney. It was founded in 2003.

There is one shop in Raharney called Weir's. They sell nearly everything you could want and really tasty ice cream. The post office is in Weir's Shop. There is one pub called McHugh's.

There is a grotto beside the bridge and the Rosary is said there every Friday in May. Across the road from the Grotto there is a little park. There are picnic benches and tables and it's a nice place to sit beside the river.

Oisin Goonery:

St. Mary's N.S., Raharney
Tel: 044 9374310
Email: reception@raharneyns.ie
Website: www.raharneyns.ie

Raharney

Raharney is a small village in Westmeath having around 231 pupils (2016 census). And is home of some cool historical monuments such as Grangemore House and St Mary's Church. The church is 188 years old and still standing! Grangemore House is said to be haunted and is visited by locals.

The River Deel is a tributary to the Boyne and flows through Raharney. Raharney also has lots of sports teams like Raharney Utd which was founded in 2003 and also a hurling/camogie team whose main rival is Clonkill. The camogie team have won the final 7 times.

It also has a school which was built in 1960. Raharney used to be a ringfort that's why in Irish it is called Rathairne. In my opinion, Raharney is a great place to live. And is a great place to start a family. It may have its flaws but also has its ups like everything else.

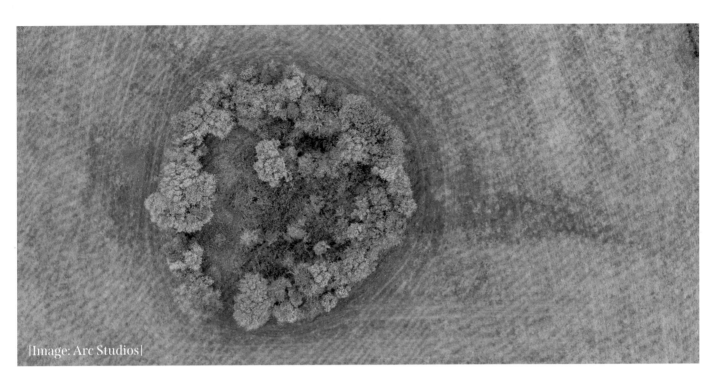

[Image: Arc Studios]

St. Mary's National School

The official name of the school is Scoil Mhuire (St. Mary's National School) but it is commonly known as Raharney National School. The School is a rural school set in beautiful surroundings about ten miles from the town of Mullingar. Mrs. Angela Farrelly is the School Principal. It is a mixed school with an enrolment of 87 pupils. There are 5 mainstream teachers & 2 Special Education Teachers.

"A Teacher's Prayer"

Lord, may I be a teacher both knowledgeable and kind.
Help me to encourage each young and growing mind.
May my faith be evident in all I say and do.
As I share the many lessons that I have learned from you.
Amen.

Raharney Schools' History

Primary education was introduced in Ireland in 1831 for Catholic children. Before this time only protestant children were allowed schooling. Many of what were called 'hedge schools' were in existence in most townlands at this time.

In the "Duchas 1939 'Schools' Collection" from Raharney school, it's believed that a school with mud walls and thatched roof existed north of where St Marys old school on the Cloughanstown Road stoof. It got its roll call No. 940 from that school. A Master Cooke, and his sister taught there. He taught

English, reading, and spellings to adults and children. His sister taught needle-work to girls and women. They lived in a little house beside the school. Teachers were paid extraordinary little then only pennies with a few drills of potatoes, and turf for fuel.

This school was in existence in 1826 and continued so for another 50 years before St .Mary's National School at Wardenstown, Raharney was built, even though Primary Education had become legal in 1831 and catholic children having been denied their basic right to education. Fr. O'Rourke petitioned the commissioners of education for new schools for the parish, as did another Parish priest on a constant basis. In 1938 James Dargan, aged 85, born 1853 of Ballinahea, stated that his father told him that a Master Curran taught 30 students in their barn, the adult students brought 1 penny a week. The only pens or pencils at the time were quills that the master dressed, and slates with lime pencils that they got in Sion Hill.

Mrs. Flanagan also from Ballinahea aged 84, born 1854, told of a Matt Gavisk going around teaching back many years before and used spend time with students on a one to one basis. A Matt Gavisk did live in Ballinahea. His name appears on the list of small holders on the Tithe list 100 years before in 1834.

After the Parish Priest petitioning the Commissioners of Education on behalf of the parents and children of the parish on a constant basis for years to have schools built, St. Mary's School was finally built at Cloughanstown, Raharney, in 1877, and served many generations of children well over the years. This was nearly 20 years after Edmonton 1858, and Rathwire 1860.

The first Principal was Mr Kelly, who taught up until 1910, when Mr Joseph Conway a native of Kildare was appointed principal and taught up until 1952. His wife was also an assistant teacher and retired in 1952. Edward O'Brien a native of Cork was appointed assistant teacher in 1910, a popular teacher who cycled daily from Edmonton for 42 years and retired in 1952. Mrs Kathleen Swords was also a long serving assistant teacher and moved to the new school in 1961.

[Image: Arc Studios]

Mr Seamus Brennan a well-respected teacher was appointed principal in 1952 and then moved to the new school in 1961. He retired in 1995. His daughter Angela was appointed and is the current principal. Mrs. Mary Farrell, assistant teacher spent most of her teaching career in St. Mary's, Raharney. Mrs. Annette Farrell assistant teacher also spent most of her teaching career in Raharney school. Many other teachers who taught over the years or presently teach in Raharney school have contributed greatly to the education of our children, and its much appreciated.

A new modern up to date school was built in Raharney in 1961 at a cost of £9,400. The architect was Mr Higginbottom and the main contractor was Mr P.F. Maguire, Athboy. By 1978 it to was deemed inadequate for the number of pupils, so new accommodation was added at a cost of £36,000. This included a general-purpose room, new classroom, cloakroom, and storage accommodation. The main contractor was Sean Dunne of Rahugh, Co. Westmeath.

A fifth teacher was appointed in 1988 the number of pupils was 145. In more recent year's additional accommodation has been added and facilities updated. St. Mary's Primary School is now a first-class school with well-behaved students and great teachers.

BELOW EXCERPTS; Taken from the Diocese of Meath: History by Fr. Anthony Cogan and Mrs. Olive Curran.

Dr Plunket noted six schools in the Parish of Killucan when he made his visitation in 1788. Eleven years later, the parson reported "There are in my parish exclusive of the district annexed to the perpetual cure three unlicenced popish schools. There are three more in the district of Kinnegad." The Report of 1826 mentions a school at Rathwire held in "a poor mud wall cabin"; a school at Raharney held in a mud wall thatched cabin, and schools at Edmonton and Ballinahee. In May 1833 Father O'Rourke petitioned the commissioners of Education on behalf of "St Mary's Seminary, Raharney," which had been established by parochial subscription in 1828. He wrote as follows :

"Honourable Gentlemen, as we are anxious to promote the moral and literary improvement of the poor children residing in the Parish of Killucan, and as there are many parents most anxious to give their children education, but they have not the means to pay for them, or even to provide suitable books of instruction for them, we are emboldened to hope that the Honourable Board of National Education will take the case of the poor of this parish into their kind and charitable consideration and extend a portion of the grant to be allocated for national education, towards the school which has sought for assistance as is within specified. We further consider that a salary of fifteen pounds per annum for the benefit of the teacher would enable him to educate the greater number of the poor children, who are residing within the distance of two miles of the school and pay one penny per week, without the slightest inconvenience to their parents. This small sum would give the children greater confidence, in point of emulation, and keep them always in the ranks of their more opulent school mates. Although there are many poor persons in the parish, the progressive state of education among the peasantry confers the highest credit on the pastors and persons, who have zealously contributed their exertions on this laudable occasion."

The Report of 1835 mentions hedge schools at Hodgestown, Ballinahee and Rathwire. National Schools were established at Edmonton 25th October 1858. Father Cogan states that until the establishment of the National Schools at Rathwire in July 1860, "there was no Catholic or National school in that portion of the Parish, owing to the narrow sectarian spirit that pervades the landlords. Although there are many poor persons in the Parish, the progressive state of education among the peasantry confers the highest credit on the pastors and persons, who have zealously contributed their exertions on this laudable occasion."

© Shay Callaghan

Priests and Religious from Raharney

Monsignor JOHN WHITE
Date of Birth: 22 July 1911. *Place of Birth:* Raharney, Killucan, Co. Westmeath. *Education:* St. Finian's College, Mullingar and All Hallows College, Dublin. *Date of Ordination:* 23 June 1935. Place: All Hallows College, Dublin. *Ordained by:* Archbishop Redmond Prendiville, Archdiocese of Perth, Australia. *Date of Death:* 3 November 1982, Aged 71. *Place of Death:* Long Beach, New York. *Burial:* Long Island National Cemetery, East Farmingdale, New York.

Rev. Fr. JOSEPH WHITE was born in Raharney, Killucan, Co. Westmeath on March 19th 1899, son of Nicholas White and Margaret McBride. He was Parish Priest of Milltown, where he passed away.

Rev. Fr. JOHN A. CUNNINGHAM was born at Riverdale, Raharney, Co. Westmeath, in 1907. He received his secondary education at St. Finian's College, Mullingar. Following his ordination at Dalgan in 1931, he was assigned to Hanyang, China. He was jailed for 15 years and deported in 1948. He returned to Ireland and did promotion work in Britain until his appointment as Director of the Irish Region in 1952. When his term as Regional Director expired, he resumed promotion work. In 1971 he took an assignment as Assistant in the Parish of Aughrim, Co. Wicklow where he died on January 1980, aged 72. He is buried at Dalgan, Co. Meath.

Rev. Fr. CHRISTOPHER CUNNINGHAM was born in Raharney, Co. Westmeath.. He was educated at St. Finian's College, Mullingar and Maynooth, Co. Kildare. Ordained on 15th June, 1915, he served in the Parishes of Johnstown, Ballinderry, Ballinabrackey, Castlepollard, Oldcastle and Nobber. He was appointed as Parish Priest in Nobber in 1936, and he moved to Dunderry, Co. Meath that same year. He died on the 14th July, 1941 aged 52.

Rev. Fr. FINIAN CONWAY was Born in Raharney, Co. Westmeath, in 1924 son of Joe Conway, the Raharney School Master. He entered the Missionary College of All Hallows in 1942, ordained for Christchurch, New Zealand in 1948. He died on 14th December 2014 aged 65 years in Christchurch after a lengthy illness. He was the sole remaining Irish priest New Zealand when he died.

Rev. Fr. JOE CONWAY was born in Raharney, Co. Westmeath and a son of Joe Conway the Raharney School Master and brother to Fr. Finian Conway, He was appointed Parish Priest of Ballymore Parish, Co. Westmeath in 1975. He loved the Irish language, and planting trees Ballymore and Boher Church grounds. He was well loved in the Parish. The new Parochial House was built in 1977 at a cost of £40,000. Fr. Joe Conway passed away on the 9th January, 1991.

Rev. Fr. CANON FRANCIS HOLDRIGHT was born in Grangebeg, Raharney, Co. Westmeath. He was educated at St. Finian's College, Mullingar and then studied at St. Patrick's College, Carlow destined for the English Diocese. He was ordained for Leeds in Yorkshire on 10th June 1928 and served from 1928-1978. During World War 2, and after the War he set about rebuilding churches and schools damaged by German bombings. He retired from St. Anne's Parish, Keighley, Yorkshire in 1973 and died in St. Francis Nursing Home, Mullingar, Co. Westmeath in 1978.

Rev. Fr. ANDREW FARRELL born on 6th September 1931. Ordained in Maynooth College 24th June 1957. He and Fr. Michael Deegan, (an uncle to our present Parish Priest, Fr. Stan Deegan) both were sent to serve in the diocese of St. Louis in the U.S.A. There they spent five years due to an over supply of priests here at home in 1957. Fr. Andrew served as teacher in St. Finian's College Mullingar and then became curate in Navan, Co. Meath until he became administrator in 1982. He served as Parish Priest in Kingscourt, Co. Cavan until 16th December 1987. In August 1994 he was moved to Trim as Parish Priest. Fr. Andrew Farrell died in Trim on 16th October 2018.

[Image: Arc Studios]

Rev. Fr. JOSEPH BENEDICT DARGAN PE left Ireland for Australia in the 1950's along with other members of his family. He worked at many jobs then followed his brother Fr. Michael Dargan into the seminary. He was ordained a Catholic priest at St. Patrick's Cathedral, East Melbourne on 21 July 1962. He served as Assistant Priest in the Parishes of Broadmeadows (1963), South Melbourne, (1965), Maidstone (1969), Seymour (1970) and Caulfield South (1974). Fr. Joe was then appointed Parish Priest at Parkville (1977) and Assistant Priest at Clayton (1978), Daylesford (1979) Belmont (1981) and Castlemaine (1982). After his appointment as Parish Priest at Meredith (1982) Fr. Joe retired in 1988 and was appointed Pastor Emeritus. His priestly ministry was witnessed through his fidelity to prayer and his gentle kindness to those he met each day. He died on Sunday August 19, 2018, at Cabrini Aged Care, Ashwood, aged 90 years. The Archdiocese of Melbourne is grateful to God for Fr. Joe Dargan's joyful, priestly witness and dedicated service to his people.

Rev. Fr. MICHAEL DARGAN was ordained a priest on 15th July 1961 and served in many parishes in Australia. He left Ireland for Australia in the 1950's along with other members of his family. Fr Michael Dargan, late of St Joseph's Home Sandgate NSW, formerly of Boolaroo, NSW Aged 93 years. Well respected member of the Catholic Clergy of the Diocese of Maitland/Newcastle and much-loved member of the local community. Fr. Michael died on 28th October 2015 and is buried in Sandgate Cemetery.

Rev. Fr. THOMAS O'MAHONY lived in Raharney from 1961 until 1971. He entered the seminary in Maynooth in 1978 and was ordained in Rathwire Church in 1985. The following 19 years were spent teaching French and Religious Education in St. Finian's College Mullingar. Fr. O'Mahony was appointed to the parish of Skryne and Rathfeigh in Co. Meath in 2005 and is still ministering there today where he enjoys his ministry.

Present Parish Priest

Rev. Fr. STAN DEEGAN is a native of Ballinagore, Co. Westmeath and was ordained in July 1992 in Castletowngeoghegan. He is now Parish Priest of Killucan/Raharney.

Religious Sisters from Raharney

Bridie North *(last of the North family in Westmeath)*, Sr. Charlotte Patricia North, Mary North.

Sr. CHARLOTTE PATRICIA NORTH RSCJ was the fifth sister in the North family from Raharney, in Co. Westmeath. She entered the Sacred Heart Convent in Dundrum, Mount Anvil Park, Dublin, at 16 years of age, leaving behind were both parents and four sisters. She was a good singer and played music and trained as a nursing sister. She was also a poet and she lives on through her poetry. She died on 20th Ocober 2013 at Our Lady's Hospice, Harold's Cross, Dublin, and she is buried in Mount Venus Cemetery, Dublin 16.

Sr. ANGELA MOONEY, (Cecilia) Raharney, joined the Congregation of the Sister's of Mercy. She was a former Matron of Tullamore Hospital, Co. Offaly. She died on 25th September 2017 and is buried in Clonminch Cemetery, Tullamore, Co. Offaly.

Sr. TESS (THERESA) SHAW along with other members of the Shaw Family (Raharney) left for Australia in 1947, by boat. The journey took six weeks. Tess joined the Sisters of St. Joseph of the Sacred Heart. She taught Religious Education in Public Schools and did not get home until after Vatican 11. She is presently in St. Camillus Nursing Centre, Killucan, Co. Westmeath.

Sr. ROSALIE RSJ CORRIGAN lived in Riverdale, Raharney with her aunts and went to Raharney National School although born in Longwood, Co. Meath. Daughter of Michael & Mary Corrigan. She left Ireland for Australia. She died on 8th March, 2021 in the seventy-first year of her Religious Profession. She is buried in Melbourne General Cemetery, Victoria.

Sr. MAY (MARCELLUS) LYNCH was born in Grange Beg, Raharney, Co. Westmeath. She attended school in Raharney then went to Freshford, Co. Kilkenny to join the Franciscan Missionaries of St. Joseph. She worked as a cook at St. Finbarr's Diocesan College at Farranferris, Co. Cork. She died at the age of 77.

Sr. ROSE CUNNINGHAM, was born at Riverdale, Raharney Co. Westmeath. She joined the Sisters of St. Joseph of the Sacred Heart, often called the "Josephites" or "Brown Joeys", were founded in Penola, South Australia, in 1866 by Mary MacKillop and the Rev. Julian Tenison Woods. Members of the congregation use the postnominal initials RSJ (Religious Sisters of St Joseph). She took Rose as her religious name. The order promoted Catholic Education in the schools throughout Australia.

Sr. NUALA CONWAY, daughter of National School Teacher, Joseph and Annie Conway, Raharney, Co. Westmeath. She joined the Sisters of Mercy, and died at their convent in Tullamore, Co. Offaly, on 27th July 2021, deeply regretted by her loving community.

Sr. Regina McHugh.

Sr. REGINA MCHUGH (BREDA MCHUGH) was born in Raharney, Co. Westmeath. She joined the Poor Clare Convent in Ennis, Co. Clare in 1983, where she spent her first year as a postulant. After that she was a novice for two years, during which she learned the rudiments of the Poor Clare life. On 29th November 1990, Sr. Regina McHugh made solemn vows, consecrating her life to God in the monastery.

Rev. Fr. Hugh Conlon

(Right) Rev. Fr. Hugh Conlon, PP. Rathwire & Raharney Parish, Co. Westmeath. Died October 1985. Buried in Rathwire Cemetery.

Rev. Fr. Richard Kesh, P.P V.F.

Rev. Fr. Richard Kelsh was a colourful character. Prior to the erection of the Parochial House in Killucan in 1880, the priests lived in a house in the parochial yard. The Parochial House (now sold) was built with the help of 1,000 pounds (old currency) obtained on loan from the Board of Works 17th. October, 1876.

However, Fr. Kelsh attained notoriety for himself in an amusing manner. " Following the introduction of the Coercion Act Fr. Kelsh wrote to Mr.A.J. Balfour, the Chief Secretary, informing him that he proposed to denounce him in both his chapels as a tyrant and a murderer. Balfour, evidently impressed, sent the letter to Dr. Nulty so that he might deal with the writer. The Bishop was no admirer of the Chief Secretary and he thoroughly enjoyed the letter and meeting Fr. Kelsh some time later he expressed the hope that he would be less blood-thirsty in his correspondence in future. Fr. Kelsh then recovered possession of the document, which he used to exhibit as a precious relic."

Rev. Richard Kelsh died in Lisdoonvarna, Co. Clare on 1st. August 1900 aged 82 and he is buried in Raharney Chapel Grounds.

|Image: Arc Studios|

The Village

Raharney (Rath Áirne) is a small village in Westmeath with a population of 519 situated on the R156 on the banks of the River Deel. It is part of Killucan Parish. Raharney's buildings and landscapes like all villages have changed dramatically over this past 60-70 years. There are still some people living, that can remember what it was like in the 40's and 50's before rural electrification came to the area in the 50's. There were no telephones nearer than Killucan until the early 50s. The village at this time was a kind of one-stop-shop, where you could purchase all items needed for daily life.

Education & Local Economy 1940's/1950's

While local employment was difficult to come by, many young people emigrated to England, some moving to Dublin to work. Local famers then were mostly self-sufficient producing their own milk, butter, eggs, oatmeal. and vegetables, while some supplied the shops with eggs and butter sometimes in exchange for other goods. Shoppers could get all their requirements in the village shops then, even if you hadn't the money, you could get it on credit, until fair day, or at the end of the week, or whenever you were paid. Shops then employed many people and were quite profitable. There is an old saying that "2 foot of a counter is better than a farm of land. Some managed to have both. Times have changed much since then, with the advent of the car, people now do most of their shopping in the bigger towns and supermarkets where there is a greater choice and keener prices.

Fianna Fáil Minister for Education, Donogh O'Malley in 1967, made second-level education free. This was reckoned to be the best decision made in Irish education. The Vocational School in Killucan, opened in 1948 and over the years developed into a progressive secondary school now called Columba College.

Webb's Shop

Webb's Bar and Grocery was a long-established business. It was inherited by Brendan Kearney in the early 1950's. Kearney ran the business for several years and built a fine house, then sold it to Frank McHugh, who together with his wife Anne ran the business successfully. This was continued by their son Loughlin and his wife Valerie until recently.

Tommy O'Reilly's

Tommy O'Reilly's Bar, General Store, Post Office and Petrol Pumps. Tommy O'Reilly, a very popular local man continued the family trade that had been passed down to him after many generations. It is now McHugh's Pub (formally known as the Granite) After he sold the business in the !970's, he built a new house across the road and continued running the Post Office and Petrol Pumps.

Garty's General Store

Garty's, the original shop and fine residence was situated across the road from Weir's present shop. This was a great shop and carried an enormous range of goods. If the customer wanted a loaf of bread, a pair of boots, shirt, a skirt, or a tyre for his bike, a gallon of oil for their lamp, a bag of flour, meal to feed their animals, all these goods and more were available in Garty's as well as in the other village shops. Garty's shop was destroyed by fire in early 1960's in which Ms. Julia Garty, one of the owners, sadly lost her life. Her sister Mrs. Rose Cunningham escaped with shock and minor injuries. Their nephew Noel Weir who worked with them, alongside his wife Una, quickly got the shop up and running again, situated across the road in a storehouse. They built it up into the fine business that it is today. In addition there is also now a Post Office and that along with the shop provides a much-needed service for the area, now run by their son Declan his wife Linda, and their son Eoin.

© Shay Callaghan

Billy Grimes

Billy Grimes was a very popular local butcher. He ran a traditional butcher's shop in Raharney. Customers came from far and near because of the high quality of his locally produced meat. His sister Nan also helped from time to time.

Nea's Shop

Nea's grocery and newsagents which was run by Mrs. Mary Nea, nee Ryan, a native of Dolla, Co. Tipperary, where her relatives were also in retail. Her husband Michael, a local man was a stone mason by trade and also had a hackney car which kept him very busy.

Mick Nea & daughter Mary.

Mick Nea, Kate, Bridie and Petee.

Holdright's Shop

Holdright's, a small shop originally started by Ciss and Josie Holdright in the 1940's as drapery, and sweet shop attached to their house, which caught fire and was destroyed in the 1970's. Their house was saved by the quick response of neighbours and the fire brigade, and no one was injured.
This house has since been purchased by Shay Murtagh who has constructed a very fine modern building called "The Third Place". This great building with fine facilities solely sponsored by Shay Murtagh is of huge benefit to the local community for meetings and social events.

Mooney's Tailors' Raharney

Mooney's were a well respected and renowned family of Tailors' in Raharney for many years. Their family business went back several generations to the 1800's. The first tailor named Mooney came from Killucan to live in Raharney with his aunt Mrs. Coughlan (nee Fulham) who had no family of her own. It was here that William Mooney from Killucan started tailoring. He married and his son Bill continued the business. Bill married Kathleen Conway and they reared three sons, Pat, Joe and Tommy who died young, and one daughter Cecelia who went on to become a nun in the Mercy Order in Tullamore. Pat and Joe both served their apprenticeship to the trade. Pat spent some time in Dublin. Joe went to England for a brief period to work in tailoring and he studied at evening classes. Both returned home to work with their father Bill, in Raharney, where the business was thriving. Customers came from a wide area, because of the good choice of materials and the exceptional quality of their tailoring with

Joe Mooney.

particular attention to detail. Many a man can recall having their First Holy Communion, Confirmation and Wedding suits made by the Mooneys'. After Bill's death, both sons continued the trade for several years. Pat married and left to start his own business in Ballinacarrigy. Joe and his wife Sheila, had four children. He continued running the business as a very professional tailor, paying close attention to style trends. He continued working up until his retirement in recent years. Joe always loved gardening and he pursued this interest until he passed to his eternal reward in December 2019. R.I.P.

Shay Callaghan

Tommy the Shoemaker

Tommy Farrelly the shoemaker's shop was situated in the Farrelly farmyard, close to the grand gates. The entrance to the old Grangemore, Estate.

Tommy was well-liked and a great craftsman. People would often visit his shop for friendly chitchat, and of course if you had shoes to be mended, however you wouldn't want to be in a great hurry with them, as he could take off fishing and you could be left waiting. His shop was full of all makes, shapes and colours of shoes and boots. Some left, that seemed to be unrepairable, and even some that had been abandoned by their owners, who had given up all hope of having them repaired. Tommy would always ensure he did a first-class job, when he got around to it.

As a highly skilled shoemaker, Tommy would make 'wax ends.' This process involved taking hemp string and covering it with wax. He would shape and roll the wax and hemp thread on his soft leather aproned lap while sitting chatting to his customers. In later years Tommy purchased a foot peddle sewing machine which was a huge help in sewing shoes.
Tommy was also a very keen and skilled angler who loved to go fly fishing on the nearby River Deel, particularly in the May-fly season. Tommy even held the record for the heaviest salmon caught on the River Deel.

Tommy was very knowledgeable and loved to talk at length about the environment, weather, local and national events, both and historical and present. His older brother Jimmy would also join in, particularly if politics was the topic of choice. Tommy and his brother were both very intelligent men. Tommy had a keen interest in nature and birds and in Spring would go to the woods close by his shop to watch and listen to the birds. If you were in his shop around Springtime, he was often heard to say "We will have an early Spring this year, the birds are threading early"

Tommy himself a bachelor, often helped his two brothers Pat and Jimmy, also bachelors on the farm. He would help with general work and haymaking and harvest time. They farmed very well in the traditional way and never changed from using the horse drawn implements and traditional methods. All tilling and mowing were done with horses including the haymaking. He was also good at baking and baked bread every couple of days, bread that would compete with the best in the land.

Tommy and his brothers lived life as God fearing people at their own pace, they always spoke well of their neighbours. They never changed their clocks or watches to summertime (now known as daylight saving time). They felt no need as their daily work was aligned with the seasons and more importantly the weather. They lived and worked in harmony with nature.

They have all since passed on to their eternal reward. RIP. Ar dheis de go raibh a anam.

© *Shay Callaghan*

The Tennis Pavilion

In 1976, the tennis courts were completed, by voluntary labour and the financial support of the community, on a site generously given by Noel Weir. After the completion of the tennis courts the club committee, chairman Shay Callaghan, Secretary Marie McHugh and Treasurer Mick Kiernan became aware of the urgent need of toilet facilities and a building to give refreshments to visiting clubs.

The club discovered a grant of £1200 was available from Westmeath County Council if the club raised a similar amount. The committee decided to avail of this grant and the only drawback was the work had to be completed before 31st Dec which meant the club had only 7 months to complete the work. The cost of the building was fixed at £2400 including ladies and gents' toilets, the installation of a septic tank and a room for refreshments.

The building was constructed on land that was part of "pudden row" which was public land outside the perimeter of the tennis courts. Furniture and some suitable equipment were given by Father Monks from The Camillians as they were changing at the time from secondary school to nursing home. Water and electricity connections were acquired from the school. A planning application to Westmeath County Council was made which caused some delay. Planning was granted by the Council, and fund raising had already commenced by way of sponsored walks, silver circle, etc. Everyone worked hard to raise money, particularly the young people of the area made great fundraising efforts.

A Credit Union loan was granted, and work commenced soon after and was completed by the 30th of Dec 1976. This loan was repaid within a short time. The Pavilion was blessed and officially opened by Father Daly C, C, that year. The tennis club committee, when it existed always made the pavilion available to any bona- fide organisations for meetings. It was also used by the school when it was short of space. It was also made available to the Midland Health Board for a few years for the Community Welfare Officer, the late Harry Devine who came once a week. This was a help to people who otherwise would have to travel to Killucan. The Health Board did make small contributions with regards this. It would be beneficial if a small committee were in place on behalf of the community to look after its maintenance and use.

As the pavilion has been grant aided by public money and repaired on many occasions by F.A.S. it cannot be used for the exclusive use of any one organisation.

© *Shay Callaghan*

Irish War of Independence

The War of Independence and Civil War was a sad and difficult time in Ireland with death and strife on a national basis, which is now 100 years ago. Only a small number of local people were very actively engaged in the actual War itself. The most notable were brothers Tom and Andy Byrne from Belview. Tom was arrested by the Black and Tans when caught carrying grenades in bags of flour on his horse's cart at Robinstown, near Ballivor, Co. Meath. The grenades were part of a large cache of arms taken when the I.R.A. burned Trim R.I.C. barracks and this was the only part of the cache ever recovered by The R.I.C.

(Left) L-R: Standing - Tom Byrne, former Old IRA member, and his brother Patsy. Sitting on the cart is Joe Lynch, name of boy unknown.

(Right) A de-commissioned Lee Enfield rifle made in 1917, used locally in the Irish War of Independence in 1920 and kept in a safe house for the past 100 years.

Tom was badly beaten and abused, and they took him home to his parents' house where they brought them both out and made them kneel and plead for their lives and threatened to shoot them all. They ransacked their house and threatened to burn it too, which at that time had a thatched roof. Tom's brother Andy, who was at the back of the house heard them coming and made good his escape. He used to say he could never sleep at home again and over the following two years he slept in sheds and safe houses around the area. Andy also felt angry that the Tans stole a new pair of boots he had just bought. Unfortunately, his brother Tom who was very badly treated and sentenced to 10 years in jail also spent over two years in Wormwood Scrubs Prison in England. He was only released when the truce came. He suffered health problems as a result and was nearly blind when he died in his sixties. However, Andy lived into his nineties and was the only local member I know of, who had a volley fired at his burial in Rathwire Cementry. This was carried out by the regular army.

On Easter Saturday 1920, Killucan R.I.C. Barracks, which was situated between the Market House and St Etchen's Church, was burned down by the I.R.A. along with the Raharney R.I.C. Barracks which was situated in what is now Harris's field between Mc Hugh's and where the late Mick Kiernan lived. Most small Barracks in the area were also burned on that night. No doubt there were many other local people who played their part in fighting for Irish Independence, like Kit Kane, Tom Goss, Jim Lennon of Mylestown and Micheal Gilsenan who lived at Knocksheban, for many years and was very active in Collinstown, Fore area, where he lived then, and many more also, the people who provided safe houses at significant risk to themselves and their families. I have been told by some, when as children, seeing strangers asleep in settle beds in their kitchens, before going to school and warned not to dare tell anyone.

© Shay Callaghan

Bord na Móna

Bord na Móna, a new semi-state company, was set up to purchase and develop bogs, and it opened its first local office in the Protestant school in Ballivor in 1946. Mr Filgate was the man in charge. Engineers surveyed Bracklyn, Lisclogher and Belview and the other bogs. In about 1950, work commenced on the construction of offices and loading facilities at Grangemore, Raharney. No planning per-mission was required then. Included in the plans were houses for employees. A small number of landowners in the Grangemore area believed the houses should, and would, be built there, close to Raharney. However, as the first office was opened in Ballivor, a lobby there succeeded in having the offices and loading bay sited there.

It was called Ballivor Works County Meath, even though it was in County Westmeath and 70% of the bogs are in Westmeath. This seems to be a good example of what lobbying can achieve. There was one drawback, the Ballivor postman did not deliver to Westmeath and a member of staff travelled to Ballivor Post Office daily to collect the post.

The building of houses for employees was a priority, and a number were built in Ballivor village, and a house for the manager nearer the works. I would think most people in both counties did not really care at the time what county the development took place in, once it happened. There is no doubt this project kept many from the emigrant ship.

Over the last 70 years, Bord na Móna created employment, part-time, full-time, and well- paid, in the Raharney, Ballivor, Delvin and surrounding areas, and the pay contributed greatly to the social and economic life of the area at a time when unemployment and emigration were high.
Many young local lads served their apprenticeships there as fitters, welders and electricians and some went on to set up their own businesses. During the summer months many whole families got employment footing and harvesting turf. Some employees spent their whole working lives with Bord na Móna, a good employer. The company still has staff, but no longer cuts turf, and in recent times stopped harvesting peat moss.

Over the years Bord na Móna received planning permission from Westmeath County Council to extend its operation at 'Ballivor Works' and it has been paying substantial commercial rates to the council over the years. This will no doubt come as a surprise to many.

The company is now in the process of looking for planning for wind turbines to produce green energy, which they claim if successful, will give further employment and improve local infrastructure such as roads and amenities such as car parks, walks and cycleways for the community.

Looking at the planned lay-out of the turbines it seems 18 of the 26 proposed, plus the substation are to be in Westmeath. According to Bord na Móna information, as they are subject to substantial commercial rates, the project would, apart from generating power also generate finance for Westmeath County Council which should be ring fenced to be spent locally.

I remember the 'Brohas', 'Derra Fluic', the New Line, and part of Bracklyn bog before Bord na Móna came in 1949 and what it was like then. We lived close by, I was 10 years old at that time and the bog was our playground then. I remember the wild raspberries and fraughans that we gathered and ate, the scent of the heather, the ferns, the bog cotton and the many different plants, the sound of birds like

Turf Cutting at Bracklyn Bog during the war 1939-1945. *(L-R)* Jack Sheils, Jimmy Flynn, Kit Greville, Jack Doyle, Andy Murray, Kit Callaghan, Joe Murtagh, Larry Poynton, Tony McManus.

Dick Lynch and Vinny Sheils.

the cackle of the grouse, the partridge, cuckoo, corncrake, curlew and skylark, also the many insects and the chirping of the grasshoppers and much wildlife that was very familiar to us as children. That was the world we lived in then.

All of that I remember clearly, but all those birds have now 'all' disappeared from these bogs with only a few remaining in the whole country. Local people came and cut their turf in the traditional way for centuries and did no harm. Recently, 71 years on. I went on a visit to a familiar but remote part of the same bog where access roads have disintegrated and almost disappeared. There were lots of birch, sally, hazel, holly trees and heather now growing. I stood and listened, just an eerie silence, even the Bord na Móna machines have gone silent. I did not see or hear a single bird. I saw two bees and three butterflies on the blossoms of plants on the roadside.

Why has this happened? Can it be repaired? This bog needs the kiss of life and to be rehabilitated. Bord na Móna promises if it gets planning permission, it will rehabilitate at least some of the bogs. I sincerely wish and hope if they get planning that they will honour this commitment.

© *Shay Callaghan*

"Two White Horses"

I spotted two white horses
In the grassy ditch
Beside the graveyard
On my way to school
Wow!

The 7th Commandment
Flashed across my fevered brain
"Thou shalt not steal"
Fearing a spooky corpse
Might rise from
The curious coffins
Their steadfast lids
Shattering the marble headstones.
"What should I do?
What should I do?"

Rhubarb sun blazing down
My vision blurred
Yes! Two shiny white horses

I ran to the church
Surely, the House of God
Would give me guidance
"What's up?" asked
The little old wrinkled-faced lady
With praying hands, noting my hysteria
As I burst through the heavy doors
She wore a scarf around her head.
"There are two white horses in the ditch" I
exclaimed,
Genuflecting in front of the tabernacle
"What should I do?
What should I do?"

"Is there anybody around?"
She whispered as if guarding my words,
"No" I answered, gasping for breath
Feeling I was in safe hands
"Bring them to me" she said wisely
I did.
"Now light a candle
To Our Lady for a nice husband."
I did.
I got one some years later.
"Light three candles for fertility"
I didn't know what that meant
I only lit one.
"Now kneel down
And pray for the person
Who lost two white horses"
I did.
With that she shoved them
Into the box beside the candles
Marked "Offerings."

Anne Maher ©

The animal chosen for the half-crown was
a horse, the coin was first struck in 1967.
Demonetised, Dec. 1969.

Coming to Raharney 1973

My first impression of those early days of 1973 when I came to live in Raharney has had lasting memories for me.

Larry Byrne of Riverdale, and Jack Gartland, also Mattie and Linda Gartland, near neighbours were the first to introduce themselves to me and welcome me into the area and wished me well. It was greatly appreciated and meant a lot to me at the time as I was a young bride struggling to find my feet in rural and village life.

I had lived and worked in the city of Dublin and due to the marriage bar had to resign from my job like most women in the Civil Service or semi-state bodies at that time, so I had all this free time which allowed me to enjoy my new rural surroundings. The village of Raharney provided everything that one needed. There were the grocery shops, the butcher, the tailor, the shoemaker, the vet, the pubs and the postmaster and they all offered a very good service.

Billy Grimes was the local butcher and I have fond memories of himself and his sister Nan. Their shop was situated on the opposite side of the road where McHugh's pub is now just a hundred yards or so on the hill. The inside of the shop was whitewashed and uncluttered. A butcher's knife, boning knife and a meat tenderiser ready for action were placed on his large wooden butcher's block. I loved to watch Billy scrub the block with his butcher's brush in the direction of the grain of the wood with slow rhythmic movements until it was cleaned to perfection. There were no sprays or chemicals that time only elbow grease which was safe in an organic environment.

Billy kept his joints of meat and sides of beef stored in the cool room or fridge for freshness. He rarely, if ever, displayed his meat in the shop. He would take my order for a round steak or whatever I fancied, and go to the fridge and carry out the side of beef. He was a strong lean man who always wore a peaked cap, and a brown shop coat while serving his customers.

Billy would sharpen his knife and place it on the side of beef and enquire what thickness I required, a decision was made after advising me that a good thick steak was best and retain the juices when cooked. I naturally took his advice as I was a novice cook in the early years and anxious to learn. However, one thing I was sure of, was that the meat was well hung, had a good colour and had a vein of fat that made it tender to eat. It was also an indication that the meat was from a beast that was out on grass, roaming the fields and had a contented life chewing the cud.

Larry Byrne.

Before Billy would proceed with my order, he would light up a fag and hold it loosely between his lips. Then with a steady hand he cut the slice to the required thickness till he reached the bone. Then he would take down the saw from the hook, take another pull of the fag, and put it back in his mouth and continue to saw over and back with the same deliberate motion as he did when he scrubbed his block. I watched the ash on the tip of his fag getting longer and longer and worried that it would fall onto the steak, but my fears were unfounded as Billy carefully took it out of his mouth in the nick of time, tapped it with his finger and again proceeded to produce a perfectly cut round steak. Then after a few whacks with the tenderiser it was ready for the ritual of the parcel. A good strong sheet of brown paper was placed on the block and the steak carefully wrapped and tied with a cotton string ready for the road. I felt I got value for money. I handled the parcel carefully as I walked the mile home as I found from experience that the juices could run and have unpleasant consequences. Plastic bags were unheard of at that time in a butcher's shop, only greaseproof and brown paper were used which were easily disposed of and had no environmental impact on the village and townlands. Billy was a gentle friendly soul and was generous with his time. He served his customers far and wide with organic meat at a very reasonable price.

On a damp day he would shake a few handfuls of saw dust on the floor to act as a non-slip surface or to soak up any spills. He had a flypaper hanging from the ceiling to catch any flies or blue bottles that dared to venture into his premises. The door was always opened, and welcoming the fresh air and conversation circulated around the shop. On days that Billy was busy in the slaughterhouse, which I try not to visualise, but it was no different in any town or village at that time, Nan, his sister was available to help out in the shop. She always had a friendly word, enquired about the family and one of her parting words of advice to me was that it was time I got a companion for the young lad in the pram." I went home and cooked up the most delicious meat and considered Nan's advice.

© *Margaret Fagan*

A Memory of Raharney

Raharney gets its name from the fort of the elder or sloes, Rath - meaning fort and Áirne - meaning sloes or elder berries. Whites in Raharney (which is now Weirs) was once a Boarding House. There was also a bakery there owned by McKenna, and an RIC barracks. The Flanagan family were also bakers. Mooneys were tailors. Murrays and Farrellys were shoemakers. Jack Cunningham was a blacksmith. Harris's were woodturners and coopers and they also made chairs, dishes, stools, butter hands, etc. Nea's were stonemasons. Ennises were dressmakers. The shops at the end of the last century were Webb's (grocery and bar), O'Reilly's (grocery, bar and post office), Garty's (grocery, drapery and hardware).

The first church in Raharney was a thatched roof and stood where James White's is now. That road was known as the street of Raharney. The present church was built in 1834. The graveyard in Raharney is called Cillholm/Kilcolumb (Colm's Church). All the old people in Raharney and the surrounding area are buried there, including Fr Swords and Fr Sherlock. Fr Swords lived in a small, thatched house on Grangemore Avenue. At one time there was a horse fair in Raharney. There were also sawmills in Raharney, owned by the O'Keeffe family and until recently, the old mill wheel and mill were exited - what a pity it is gone. In the latest century there was a turnpike at Joristown at which tolls were collected, which was used to improve roads. At that time, the roads were maintained by the Grand Jury - mostly landlords.

A number of men from the area fought with the British Army in the First World War. A list of those killed are in St Etchen's Church, Killucan. Some privates in the war from the area were Walter Carroll, Paddy L'Estrange, Paddy McKenna, Jack Fleeson, Paddy Brennan, Paddy Doyle, the last two were not in the war. A lot of recruiting went on at the fair and markets. If they decided to join, they were given a shilling and then they were committed men. There was a place in Delvin called the Dardanelles because of all the men there who fought in the First World War.

The River Deel flows through Raharney and has often lent its name to the hurling team, who are often called "the Deelsiders." That hurling team is in Raharney since it was formed by a Leix man in 1885, and it has almost been continually in existence since Raharney didn't suffer greatly from the famine, although times were pretty lean. During the Famine years, it was said people came from fifty to sixty miles away, to get work on the Deel, as it was deepened then to give relief work. Some who travelled so far, got neither work nor food and died there and were buried at the Deelside. Some years ago, a large number of human bones were found there (in Purdon's wood near the river). The bridge in Raharney was used during the Famine, there were five arches under it. People lived under the bridge. One such family was the "Hamilton's." There was a soup kitchen in operation during the famine.

There are interesting remains of a church in Kilcolumb Graveyard. There is also the remains of a graveyard and church in Kilaheen. Mostly unbaptised children were buried there. Tradition has it that there were bishops buried there too. The graveyard is on Grangemore land. There were two roads from Raharney to Ballivor, the old road stretched from Dunphy's to Donnelly's. The new road went from Webb's to Dunphy's. The old road was used up to the mid-last century. Grangemore House was built around 1811 by Captain Briscoe. During that time, until the Famine in Black '47, things were relatively quiet in Ireland. At one time, there was a windmill on Grange Avenue, just on the hill above Farrelly's house. There was an old mud building alongside to where Raharney's St Mary's National School was built in 1877. This old cabin was used as a hedge school and Master Doyle taught there.

Famous Raharney names: Christopher Murray from Raharney was an important man in the Westmeath Association in New York. George Flanagan was Mayor of Boston. He died around 1940. John Darcy, my ancestor, was Lord Mayor of Dublin.

© *The Late Nell Geoghegan*

Kitty Mulvaney & Maureen Donoghue. [Image: Arc Studios]

Bill Raleigh Postman: 1924-1974

Daily life for the women and men of Raharney Village could have been very mundane, a time before post-vans, phones or emails, but NO! They had Bill Raleigh. For fifty years he travelled around the village delivering much anticipated parcels from America, love letters from the four corners of the country and even the dreaded bills. He cycled from house to house always with a smile on his face and could be heard chatting away to himself as he went about his business. R.I.P Bill, and thank you for your dedicated years of service.

© Lillie Connaughton

Hughie & Mary Flanagan

This brother and sister duo lived in the heart of the village and whilst they went about their daily lives in a quiet unobtrusive manner, they were ahead of their time with their organic farming business. Hughie grew a wide variety of fruit and vegetables, and every Friday would bring the produce to sell at the Mullingar Market. Mary made the most wonderful jams, often experimenting with different combinations, but her signature product was her plum jam, made from the most delicious plums that grew on a tree in their front garden. If there was a Michelin Star for jams, Mary would have got a 5!

© Lillie Connaughton

Mary Flanagan & Paddy Nolan.

Paddy & Jimmy Nolan with Hughie Flanagan.

Thomastown Mill

The importance of milling in Raharney and the surrounding areas is evident from the significant efforts the local people put into the survival of Thomastown Mill, which following the closure of Raharney Mill was essential for the farming community. Shares were sold to people for miles around in Raharney, Warenstown, Craddenstown, Riverdale, Grangebeg, Ballinahee, Clonboor etc..

The Department of Agriculture and Technical Instruction introduced a scheme of compulsory tillage in 1917. This part of Westmeath did not have the required milling facilities which had the potential to cause great hardship to farmers in the area. In 1918, Killucan Milling Society Ltd purchased the kilns, mill, the plot of land enclosing them (about 1 acre statue) and the existing Water Rights for £300.00 from Mr.

Price. The mill situated in Cushenstown, known as Thomastown Mill was visit by engineers from both the Department of Agriculture and the IAOS (Irish Agricultural Organisation Society) who *expressed the opinion that 'The mill walls are sound and good, that the kiln is in repair, that the water power is ample for a 25 H.P turbine and generally that the building and appurtenance are well worth the sum agreed upon to be paid to Mr Price.'

To fund the running of the mill, Killucan Co Operative Milling Society Limited shares were sold for £1 each. On the 21st of May 1918, a meeting was held for the purpose of allotting shares. There were applications for 777 shares from 224 subscribers, subsequently further shares were sold and cancelled. The *records show the following list-

LIST OF SHAREHOLDERS

NAME	*S	NAME	*S	NAME	*S
Colonel Purdon Winter, Lisnabin	50	Joseph Forde, Knockmant	3	John Colgan, Craddenstown	1
A.T.F. Briscoe JP Co C	25	Patrick Dunne, Ballyhaw	3	Thomas Bray, Craddenstown	1
Joseph Creevy, St. Joseph's Parochial Hse. Killucan	25	Nicholas White D.C. Raharney	3	Michael Larrigan, Craddenstown	1
Francis Gilsenan, AnnisKannan	20	Bartle O'Reilly, Raharney	3	Edward Connor, Porterstown	1
James Ross, JP Co C Moyvalley	10	John Allen, Derrymore	3	Mrs Jamie Dixon, Killyon N.S.	1
R.F. Wilson, Sion Hill and Bray	10	William Kellaghan, Cloncrave	3	Edward Gaffney, Croboy	1
Miss A.K Harris, Moore's Hotel, Killucan	20	James Colgan, Griffenstown	3	Edward Larrigan, Ballasport	1
James Webb, Raharney	10?	Edward Sheridan, Griffenstown	3	Mrs M Leavy, Croboy	1
Peter Keegan, DC Balroan	10	John Oxley, Cloncrave	1	Michael Casserley, Croboy	1
Miss Jane Webb, Killucan	10	James Quinn, Thomastown	2	Thomas Dixon, Mt Hevey	1
Mrs. F.B Purdon, Huntingdon Ho.	10	John Duffy, Riverstown	2	Patrick Healy, Ballasport	1
Andrew Dunne, Riverbank	10	James Crinion, Cushenstown	2	Frank McBride, Clondalee	1
J. P. Garty, DC, Raharney	10	Christopher Glennon, Porterstown	2	Richd Quinn, AnnisKannan	1
William Price, Rathwire	10	Mrs E. Browne, Edmonton	2	Mrs M Flanagan, AnnisKannan	1
Thomas Price, Rathwire	10	Jeremiah Gibson, Grangebeg	2	Mrs J Bray, Clonboor	1
Michael Ward, Croboy	10	James Gaffney, Ballyhaw		John J Leavy, (Senior) Knockmant	1
R.E. Hickey, Hydepark	10	Christopher Dunne, Hyde Park	2	James Goonery, Rathras	1
Christopher Connor, Sarsfieldstown	6	Hugh O'Reilly, Killyon	2	Christopher Dixon, Killyon	1
John Heffernan, Cushenstown	6	Andrew Gorman, Knockmant	2	Thomas Lynam, Raharney	1
Thomas Cleary, Ballinla	5	Mrs B. Cunningham, Rathwire	2	Peter McKeogh, Derrymore	1
Patrick Quinn, Edmonton	5	Christopher Flanagan, Croboy	2	Bernard Coakley, Croboy	1
Christopher Cunningham, RiverDale	5	Mrs B. Kavanagh, Derrymore	2	James Massey, Derrymore	1
Patrick Keegan, Rathwire Lower	5	Joseph Leavy, Croboy	2	Thomas Geraghty, Derrymore	1
Edward Cole, Riverstown	5	James Hannon, Clondalee	2	Mrs. D Cunningham, Clondalee	1
James McKeogh, Croboy	5	Thomas Corcoran, Knockmant	2	Patrick Cunningham, Clondalee	1
Joseph Coyne, Ballinlig	5	Michael Kelly, Grehanstown	2	Thomas O'Neill, Craddenstown	1
Christopher Quirke, Inan	5	John Carroll, Balroan	2	Thomas Harris, Grange Beg	1
Michael Peppard, Croboy	5	Patrick Leavy. Balroan	2	Peter Hetherston, AnnisKannan	1
James Glennon, Joristown	5	Wm Bailey, Killucan	2	Mrs W. Rowan, New Down	1
Nicholas Quirke, Clondalee	5	Peter Smith, Killucan	2	James Carley, New Down	1
Christopher Hevey, Hill of Down	5	Mrs. M. Kiernan, Croboy	2	Christopher Murtagh, The Downs	1
Michael Gorman, DC Knockmant	5	Andrew Dunne, Derrymore	2	Thomas O'Hara, Knockmant	1
Mrs. M. Cleary, Riverstown	5	Maurice Whelehan, Derrymore	2	Patrick Faulkner, New Down	1
Mrs. B. McKeon, Greenhills	5	James Leavy, Derrymore	2	Thomas Hughes, Hyde Park	1
William Lee, Rathwire	5	Patrick Keegan, Derrymore	2	James Hanlon, New Down	1
James J. Jackson, Killucan	5	John Slevin, Derrymore	2	Richard Corroon, New Down	1
Rev B.S Radcliffe, B.D. Killucan	5	John White, Ballinlig	2	Patrick Gaughran, Hyde Park	1
Mrs. Ellen Meares, Killucan	5	James Farrell, Clonboor	2	Mathew Brock, Hyde Park	1
Patrick Whelehan, Derrymore	5	Francis D'Arcy, Corbetstown	2	Patrick Hughes, Derrymore	1
Andrew Holdright, Grange Beg	5	Francis Fagan, Corbetstown	2	Matthew Carroll, AnnisKannan	1
James Carbery, Hyde Park	5	Patrick Corroon, Knockmant	2	Joseph Mitchell, Hyde Park	1
Andrew Kellaghan, Great Down	5	Joseph Leavy, Castle Down	2	Edward Reilly, Brutonstown	1
C.T.B. Vandeleur, Wardenstown	5	John Flynn, New Down	2	Miss Lucy Mitchell, Hyde Park	1
Thomas Colgan, Knockmant	5	James Hughes, Hyde Park	2	Thomas McNally, Knockmant	1
Patrick Lynam, Porterstown	5	Charles Fagan, River Dale	2	Edward Flynn, Knockmant	1
Patrick Cunningham, Riversdale	5	Christopher Fox, Curristown	2	Mrs. Mary Lynam, Knockmant	1
Philip Dunne, Cloncrave	5	Mrs A Gilligan, Croboy	2	Peter Kilduff, Joristown	1
James Garty, Brutonstown	5	Richard Clarke, Derrymore	2	Christopher Cunningham, Joristown	1
Andrew O'Keeffe, Priestown	5	Thomas Kiernan, Inan	2	Hugh Lamb, Joristown	1
John O'Neill, Corbetstown	5	James Connolly, Clondalee	2	Wm Grimes, Curristown	1
Mrs Scally, Lewinstown	5	Francis Malone, Clondalee	2	John Anderson, Wardenstown	1
Michael Ward, Scarden	5	Matthew Shaw, Riverdale	2	Hugh Reilly, Ballyhaw	1
Thomas Scally, Priestown	5	Wm Doyle JP Cloncrave	2	William O'Neill, Raharney	1
Thomas O'Reilly, Simonstown	5	Patrick Keogan, Thomastown	2	Thomas O'Keeffe, Grange Beg	1
Edward Holdright, Wadestown	5	Patrick Quinn, Thomastown	2	Edward Dargan, Rathras	1
Peter Flynn, Creggstown	5	Mrs Rose Coffey, Newtown	1	Clement Bates, Derrymore	1
Thomas O'Keeffe, Porterstown	5	Edward Slevin, Cushenstown	1	Robert Coyne, Croboy	1
James G. Potterton, Craddenstown	5	Thomas Giles, Porterstown	1	Joseph McBride X Rds Clondalee	1
Patrick Coffey, Thomastown	5	Robert Dunbar, Grehanstown	1	James Cole, Killyon	1
Mrs Kate Donnellan, Thomastown	5	Peter Corcoran, Porterstown	1	Patrick Dixon, Killyon	1
Michael Magill, Porterstown	4	Mrs McGarry, Grehanstown	1	Edward Kelly, Wardenstown	1
Maurice Keeffe	3	Wm Kelly, Grehanstown	1	Edward Gilligan, Riversdale	1
Nicholas Barden, Grehanstown	3	Owen Murray, Porterstown	1	Patrick Maguire, Rathras	1
Arthur Coffee, Hodgestown	3	Peter Judge, Grehanstown	1	Edward Lynch, Rathras	1
Thomas Murray, Riverstown	3	Michael Flanagan, Craddenstown	1	Andrew Lynch, Grange Beg	1
Nicholas Judge, Banagher	3	Mrs. Simon Ludlow, Edmonton	1	Michael Glynn Thomastown	1
Francis O'Keeffe, Craddenstown	3	John Fetherston, Edmonton	1	Thomas Bennett (Snr) Cloncrave	1
James Mangan, Mill Park	3	Matthew Staunton, Edmonton	1	Patrick Dunne Nil	20
Joseph McBride, Clondalee	3	Thomas Anderson, Ballyhaw	1	Luke Nolan, Derrymore Nil	20
Christopher Flynn, Rathwire	3	Denis Gaffney, Ballyhaw	1	Nicholas Sharry, Killucan	
Patrick Seery, Banagher	3	Patrick Webb, Grange Beg	1	Thomas Bennett DC. Cloncrave	5
James McKeon, Killucan	3	James Flynn, Lewinstown	1	Patrick J Oxley, Derryboy	3
John Carroll, Sarsfieldstown	3	Laurence Casserley, Hyde Park	1	J Kilmartin D.C. Kinnegad	5
Thomas Bracken, Killucan	3	Peter Keegan, Hyde Park	1	Thos Cole Farmer Hyde Park	5
Michael Brien, Killucan	3	James Leech, Hyde Park	1	Mrs. Mary A. Lennon, Riverstown	2
John Coakley, Derrymore	3	Patrick Lynch, AnnisKannan	1	James Hill, Thomastown	1
Mrs. Anne Bruton, Derrymore	3	Patrick Corcoran, Craddenstown	1	**228**	

*S = Number of Shares

Mr. A.T F. Briscoe Esq. J.P. acted as Chairman, with Mr. Peter Keegan D.C. Treasurer and the Secretary appointed for the Co-op was Mr. Thomas Murray.

The building contract was awarded to Mr. Thomas O'Reilly Simonstown. J.E Wallace Esq. Solicitor acted for the Co-op in legal matters.

It was hoped that the mill would be up and running by December 1918. However, during this period of political and economic unrest there were setbacks and disappointments for the Co-op. The machinery was not delivered within the arranged timeframe, there were delays erecting the machinery and problems with the plan of the machinery supplied by the I.A.W.S (Irish Agricultural Wholesale Society). At a meeting on the 7th of May 1920, the Secretary Mr. Murray was asked to write to Mr. Wallace, Solicitor for the Co-op, and instruct McGrath to vacate the Mill House. Mr. Thomas Coffee was to be taken on as Miller on a week's trial, on a weekly wage of £3.00, to include board, lodgings and travel. At a meeting on the 3rd of June 1920 the Secretary Mr. Murray was asked to write to Mr. Coffee saying that the Co-op no longer wanted him as they had made other arrangements.

The Co-op then appointed Mr. W. O'Brien as miller to work the mill until July, to be paid £4.00 weekly while the mill was working and £2.00 when the mill was idle, with a lodging allowance of five shillings a week in lieu of his house. The mill house was to be put into proper habitable conditions.
Mr. James McCauley took over as miller in 1921.

At the General Meeting of the Shareholders held on the 17th of July 1922, a condolence was expressed to Mrs. O'Reilly of Simonstown on the passing of Mr. Thos. O'Reilly 'a good worker and good friend to the shareholders and the mill as a tribute of respect to his memory his son Mr. James O'Reilly was unanimously appointed to the Committee of Management'.

(Left) Westmeath Examiner (1882-current) Saturday, 19th September 1925.

(Right) Westmeath Examiner (1882-current) Saturday, 22nd October 1921.

At the General Meeting held on September 1931, the wages of the staff were reduced. The Miller and the Secretary received £2.5.0 each the Kiln man £1-17-6 per week.

The mill continued to operate successfully into the 1950's. In 1953 it was purchased by Mr. Jim Coyne who continued to operate the Mill up until the 1960's.

As the demand for mills declined the building fell into a derelict state. It was purchased by Billy Boyle from Raharney in 1998. After some difficulty with planning permission ,Billy finally restored the mill with great diligence, retaining as many original features as possible to a beautiful residential property. Bill did this over a period of 2 years taking his time to considering each unique feature.

Aerial View of Raharney

1	Site of Mill	7	McKenna's Bakery 1920
2	Site of Castle	8	Mick Kiernan
3	Rivervalley Mushrooms	9	RIC Barracks
4	Tennis Court	10	M. Webb Dispensary
5	School	11	Josie's Now 3rd Place
6	The Island Park		

Tom Ivory - Blacksmith in 1949

As the school clock chimes three it means school is over for today. Owen feels like making a dash for the door to get out before Jimmy, who always gets to Tom Ivory's the blacksmith's forge before Owen, but he suddenly remembers Jimmy isn't in school today. He was kept at home to help his father pick the spuds.

This means Owen can take his time now. There was always competition between Jimmy and himself to blow the bellows for old Tom Ivory the blacksmith, who was now getting on a bit and finding it hard to get around, with the 'auld pains' as he would say himself. His mode of transport is Neddy, his ass and cart which takes him the half mile to the village, to get his groceries and a few pints of stout which he enjoys very much. The front transom of the cart is easy and handy to sit up on and he lets his legs hang down. Neddy the old ass knows the way quite well.

When Owen got to the forge, situated about half a mile from the school on the Craddenstown road, beside Tom's cottage, and surprisingly is constructed of wood including the roof that is painted with a black tar-like paint to keep out the rain. There is no door, and its rather dark inside which gives the iron, when hot a much redder glow. Tom was busy making a set of shoes for Pat Farrelly's Clydesdale horse which was a very big horse with hairy legs and big hooves. Tom seemed to be glad to see Owen arrive as he could do with any little help he could get. The big bellows was made of leather with a pole and a short piece of rope on the end hanging down. The pole runs back over another pole to give leverage to make it easy to pull. Owen pulls hard on the rope which he can barely reach, the fire soon starts to redden up.

The red glow from the fire reflects off Tom's face and forehead, where a few beads of sweat are beginning to appear as he stokes the fire and puts in the iron. After a short while Tom removes the red-hot iron from the fire with a long-handled tongs, and puts it on the anvil, he then strikes it hard sending a shower of sparks in all directions. Owen now stands and watches, fascinated by a master of his craft at work, with a lifetime of experience. The ring from the hammer as it hops on the cold anvil and the sort of dull sound as it strikes, the red-hot iron, which Tom reheats many times, as he bends strikes and shapes to get an exact copy of the horseshoe hanging on the peg. Finally, he now punches the holes for the nails, and dips it in a tub of water with a loud hissing sound to cool and hangs it on a peg. To be greatly admired by Owen, who thinks it's a work of art. Tom will repeat the process three more times. But Owen now thinks it is time to head for home. Tomorrow is another day when he will again visit Tom's forge and see him fitting the shoes. The following day his friend Jimmy is still at home from school picking the spuds which means Owen will be able to visit the forge unhindered again today to blow the bellows and help Tom.

As school now ends, Owen quickly makes his way to the forge looking forward and hoping to see Pat Farrelly's Clydesdale horse getting his new set of shoes. Pat Farrelly has just arrived with the horse which is even bigger than Owen imagined. Blacksmith Tom's upper body strength is still quite good as he lifts the big hooves and pulls it up between his knees and gets to work, first removing the old shoe, cleaning and paring the big hoof with a special knife with a sort of hook on the end of it.
Tom gives Owen the nod to start blowing the bellows, the fire soon reddens up, Tom takes the shoes that he made yesterday from the hook and puts them in the fire to heat up. After a short while he removes the red hot shoe from the fire and places it on the horses hoof filling the forge with a fog of smoke with a very strong smell of burning hoof, which after careful fitting it is soon nailed on with the special horse shoe nails that are clinched and smoothed off with the big rasp. This is repeated three more times and the big horse now stands proud in his new set of shoes. Owen must now run for home as he has been warned by his mother many times not to be dallying coming from school.

© Shay Callaghan

Raharney Mill and Castle

Raharney in 1650 was then called Rathfarne and was a very busy place with its own castle in the village in good repair. According to Westmeath Co. Council the Castle was sited between the Mooney's and Callaghan's houses. The castle in Grangebeg, also in good repair at that time, was sited where Gibson's house stands. Maybe there are some remains there now. A sketch of both castles appears on the Down Survey map of that time. According to Lewis's Topographical Dictionary of Ireland 200 years later in 1837 it states that adjoining the village are only the remains of an old Castle with walls extending across the river. Now however another 200 years later again there is no trace of any castle there.

A waterwheel driven mill on the River Deel also appears on the Down Survey in 1650. This mill was used to mill grain to make oatmeal that was in high demand by most of the population to make porridge and bread. This meal was also used extensively in the feeding of livestock and fowl. A corn Kiln was also on the site for drying the grain. A corn market took place in village every Tuesday at which a large amount was sold. A section of the mill was also used as a tuck mill. A tucking mill is used in the making of cloth from wool by pounding the woollen cloth or fulling as it was called. The wool had first to be washed, carded, and then spun and loosely woven into a cloth which was called Frieze. This was a very hard-wearing cloth and would last for years. There is no doubt this created much needed employment for women and girls.

A wool market took place on a regular basis. The land is described in the Down Survey as good quality meadows with good sheep walks. Sheep and wool production seem to be the most common type of farming carried on then. Surveys also show that a breed of black cattle were also farmed extensively on some farms.

In later years the mill was also used as a timber sawmill. Many houses in the area had roof timbers sawn in this mill. The mill was in constant use for over 400 years and closed in 1945. However, prior to this it seems no corn was milled there for several years. It was only used for sawing timber A 1917 Survey of Corn Mills in Westmeath show that Josephs O 'Keefe's corn mill in Raharney, Andrew Connelly's corn mill Balrath, Killucan, Ms. Mary Hegarty's corn mill Kilough, Bracklin, were all 'unused with some machinery' and Hannon's Mill Killucan, described as 'skeleton mill'.

The nearest working corn mill to Raharney / Killucan was James Flynn's Mill, Hightown, Coralstown. This was the only mill working and was quite a distance for most farmers. The lack of a corn mill locally was a considerable disadvantage for famers to have to travel long distances to have grain milled. Thomastown Mill that was not mentioned in the survey of 1917 which seems strange but seeing this Mill had been working for many years as a corn mill, and tuck mill was generally used in the making of cloth from wool. However, there was great need for a corn mill in this area, therefore farmers would support any effort in getting a mill up and working.

About this time 1918, Thomastown Mill Co-op Society was formed and purchased Thomastown Mill and approx. I acre of surrounding land from Mr Price for £300. Nearly every farmer in Raharney and Killucan Parish and beyond, bought shares which were £1 each and some bought many shares. About this time discussions between Westmeath County Council the Department of Agriculture and Technical Instruction, a scheme of assistance was approved commencing in 1917, whereby the Department made loans available direct to mills that were recommended by the Council for repair and new equipment. Interest free loans were given to these mills The County Council took responsibility for the interest over a ten-year period.

Initially however no grant appears to have been given to Thomastown Mill. Some mention of a grant of £400 does appear later. Due to the fact no local mill was working locally or within a reasonable distance particularly in the Raharney area to mill corn, the Thomastown co-op was fully supported by 220 people purchasing shares by farmers and non-farmers. A hard-working committee was set up and the mill building, and the millers house were fully refurbished including the kiln and coal store. New equipment was purchased and installed and the water systems up graded. This work encountered some difficulties and took a couple of years to complete. On completion of this work the mill was a great success and served the local community very well over many years up until the early fifties. There were a few millers employed over these years Patrick Carroll of Rathwire who trained Barney Murtagh, a very popular miller for many years until it closed in 1953. The mill was purchased by Jim Coyne who continued milling corn with tractor power until the seventies when it finally closed.

Sluice Gate and Salmon Leap
RAHARNEY, CO. WESTMEATH

Raharney mill is believed to have continued sawing timber until 1945, when it finally closed. A few older people remember when the Raharney Mill was in operation and the sluice gate on the dam closed and most of the water redirected into the millrace to power the Mill. This water would re-emerge again into the main river in the Island. With little water now remaining in the main river for about 200 yds. the children going home from school and locals alike could fish by hand and catch some nice trout to bring home for dinner. The Mill and dam were very sound well-built stone structures and remained intact until demolished and buried without trace by the O.P.W. when draining the River Deel in 1975/6. I witnessed this at the time and felt how could the O.P.W. a semi state body that looked after old castles and heritage buildings do this. It certainly would not be allowed to happen now. This together with the deepening of the riverbed lowering the water table by over 2 meters, (O.P.W. figures), and closing the millrace had a dramatic effect on all fish stock and plant life on the river and totally changed the surrounding landscape. As 1975/6 were very dry summers, and all wells in the area dried up.

As a result of this a voluntary group water scheme was set up by locals, and grant aided by the Dept of Local Government to bring water to the village, which was completed in 1979.
The O.P.W. left the area in a mess. I built a retaining stone wall along my garden boundary.
The mayfly almost disappeared. Now nearly 50 years on there is some little improvement.
My house and garden border the river and dam and I remember missing the pleasant and relaxing sound of the water flowing over the weir (dam) on a calm night before the weir and mill were demolished.

I watch with interest now every year for the small number of mayflies. As they rise to the surface from the bed of the river and emerge from their cocoons to be picked off by the very few trout that are there now, this in competition with the swallows, house martins, and particularly the wagtails, that do some aerobatic flying to get their share. The flies that make it to the bushes and find a mate and return to lay their eggs and start the circle all over again are rare and the extremely lucky ones. The Kingfisher has returned in the last few years. Its food source must also have returned, This must auger well for the future. The trees, plants and bushes have regrown somewhat, and I would say the river has sort of healed up for want of a better description.

© Shay Callaghan

The Office of Public Works (OPW) is a government office that manages public government properties and heritage services.

The Island

The Island as it has always been known, back many years ago was an area of land which was then part of the mill owner's property, where the mill race ran on one side and the River Deel on the other. The mill, which was a particularly important part of the local economy, over many centuries was situated 100 meters up stream on the river Deel. It was sometimes used as a place where the traveling shows used visit occasionally in the 1940's and 1950's.

To see the show people erecting their tent and equipment, brought great excitement and joy into the lives of the children, as they arrived down on their way home from school, it was thrilling to see the swinging boats and other amusements in action. They would rush home to tell their parents and beg to be brought to see the show.

Over the years the travelling shows stopped coming and during the cleaning of the river in 1975 a lot of spoil was dumped on the Island which made the surface rather rough. The Tidy Towns Committee did what they could to maintain and improve its appearance.

It was here with great excitement that the big bonfire was lit in 1984, the centenary year of the G.A.A. When the Raharney Hurling club done a clean sweep in the hurling championship from senior right down to minor.

The Island changed ownership a couple of times around this time. As Chairman of Westmeath County Council in 1990-91 I had the opportunity to get the Council to purchase the Island and to have it put in public ownership as a lineal park for the village, which was successful. I was also lucky in getting Richie Mc Cabe from the drawing office to draw up plans for developing the Island and putting a footpath behind the existing road boundary wall, to make it safer for pedestrians. Most of this plan was implemented by social employment schemes over the years, and by a very hard-working Tidy Towns Committee. It was mostly members who lived outside the village, working with good skilled supervisors. This effort is ongoing, even since, more fantastic work has recently been carried out by the Tidy Towns Committee, which is grant aided and supported by the Community Development Section of Westmeath Co Council.

The Island now is a pleasant and lovely place to come for locals and visitors alike, to sit and enjoy the flowers, plants, the river and nature. With great credit due to the local community and all the people that have been involved over many years. Our future hopes would be to improve the footpath across the bridge, to aid safe passage of pedestrians.

© Shay Callaghan

Raharney Dispensary

Raharney Dispensary was held in Mick and Mrs. Webb's, an old, thatched farmhouse, which was situated about 100 meters on the left-hand side out the Riverdale Road. The house was very dark inside with only small windows. Patients waited in the kitchen beside a good turf fire and were seen by the Dr in the parlour. The house has long since been demolished.

Dr. Cox attended every Tuesday from 10am to 1pm. Facilities in the dispensary at that time were poor, no electricity, running water, just a jug of water, basin, and a clean towel. With just the basic Doctor's equipment and a good torch which he shone down the patient's throat, or anywhere else he wished to view. He thoroughly examined each sick person and with his years of experience could learn a lot about their state of health by examining their tongue, eyes, pulse, blood pressure, and temperature. If the patient had an infection, he would give a Penicillin injection in the backside which generally was not looked forward to by the patient.

With many years of medical experience Dr. Cox looked after his clients very well and did house calls 24 /7. People at that time went to see a doctor only when necessary and generally had to pay. There were many living in the area at that time who had cures for various ailments including ringworm, jaundice, burns. and many more complaints. Some were very old remedies made up of herbs mixed with unsalted butter into a sort of ointment. Those were found to be quite good. Some people only went to the doctor after trying the home remedies without much success. There is a true story told about a local man called Andy who arrived at Dr. Cox's dispensary one day. "Well Andy what's the matter" asks Dr Cox? "Well," says Andy "They tell me I don't look well at all" "I see!" says the Doctor, "You look fine to me Andy" "O.K. so!" Andy then turns on his heel, and on the way out he meets Mick coming in who inquired as to how Andy was. "I am fine now" replied Andy, "I am just after getting all clear."

Mick Webb.

In the 1940's Tuberculosis or T.B. as it was commonly known, was very prevalent in the locality and was a very contagious and a dreaded disease that had in the past wiped out whole families. Around this time a cure mostly believed by way of penicillin was found and most patients were now surviving this awful disease. Around the early 1950's, several cases of polio were diagnosed in the parish. This was a serious disease and could be fatal and caused great worry to the families concerned and the wider community. Immunisation of children against both diseases commenced in the schools. The 'Home Assistance Officer' as he was then known, called to the dispensary in the afternoon. Only people who had hit on hard times, or in poor health, with large families called for some assistance. Generally, some was given.

© Shay Callaghan

The Hall, Raharney

The Hall in Raharney was situated where the school and church carpark is now. In the early fifties with good encouragement from Fr. Delaney our C.C. who was great to get things done, got a small group together and erected what was really a Nissen hut type building. Matt Gartland was detailed to collect the hall in Cavan on his truck. He also later did the electric wiring.

It was erected by the Late Liam Geoghegan, Jimmy Rooney, Mick Nea, together with other voluntary helpers. Block walls were built with a concrete floor and cast-iron stove for heating. It was a substantial building and from memory I would guess it was about 50 foot long by 25 wide.

You could say it was built in the fifties and knocked in the sixties, together with the hopes of the young people, of any opportunity of socially getting together or enjoyment. I am sure many people have fond memories of the Tuesday nights film shows back then. And quite a few romances did blossom there. The hall was used extensively for meetings, card playing, and the showing of films. Mrs Murray from

Killmessan, Co. Meath gave films shows every Tuesday night, which was very much looked forward to by the local boys and girls.

Travelling shows came from time to time. Courtneys was one show that filled the hall every night for a couple of weeks.

It was decided by whom I don't know to demolish the hall for provision of a Church and school carpark around 1967. This carpark was needed, but not at the expense of the local hall as a result there was no place to have meetings and entertainment.

 Architecturally it was not pretty but served a great need. An alternative could and should have been found. The steel remains of the hall are still to be found in Kit Greville's garden.

The Nissen Huts were named after Major Norman Nissen (6th August 1871 – 2nd March 1930) a Canadian Engineer serving with the British Army, who designed them in the summer of 1916 for World War 1. They were a prefabricated building of corrugated steel in the shape of a half cylinder. They were temporary structures which were economical, portable and quickly assembled. They were constructed mainly for military use to shelter troops in the First World War. Especially useful as a barracks, they were adapted throughout the war to suit different requirements including an extremely popular Hospital version. They had concrete floors and at first, people complained that they were freezing cold and drafty in the winter and far too hot summer. However, in 1917, the Hut was redesigned using non-combustible insulation. At least 100,000 Nissen Huts were produced including 10,000 Hospital version. Then in 1939-1945 large numbers were produced again for the Second World War.

In 2017, there was a renewal project. It was an opportunity to show how these modest little shacks could be adapted and modernised. They updated the Hut to meet the current code of standards and to provide more comfort and flexibility inside. I particularly would like this office in my garden.

© Shay Callaghan

Chernobyl

The Chernobyl nuclear disaster, which has been described at the United Nations as 'the worst environmental catastrophe in the history of humanity' took place on 26th. April 1986, at the Chernobyl Nuclear Power Station in the Northern Ukraine. Following an explosion at Reactor No. 4, 190 tons of radioactive materials were released into the atmosphere. At least 9 million people have been affected by the disaster.

1996-2006

Over these past ten years the people of Killucan/Raharney/Kinnegad opened their hearts and their homes to welcome over thirty-three children and three adult translators for one month's rest and recuperation from their radioactive contaminated environment. The local people volunteered a lot of time and energy to fundraise this programme. Doctors, nurses, dentists, nurses, opticians, shops, restaurants, and cafes and all contributed to the children's wellbeing. The host families joined in, taking weekly outings to places like Glendeer Pet Farm, Athlone, Fort Lucan, Dublin Zoo, Butlin's Mosney Holiday Camp, The Imax Cinema in Dublin, The National Wax Museum in Dublin, Clonmacnoise and West Offaly Railway Bog Train, Mullingar Equestrian Centre, Killure Candle Making, to mention a fe, not forgetting Henry Slaone (R.I.P.) of the 'Jolly Mariner' making sure we always got a trip on the River Shannon each year. The children received a Cead Mile Failte everywhere.

Setting Out For Russia

The committee also organized the sending out of three ambulances with local drivers, driving across Europe to the Chernobyl affected regions. They drove in convoy, an approximate total of 3,000 miles. The drivers were Kevin O'Neill (Millarstown) Barry Rogers (Coralstown) Tony Murtagh (Raharney) Jimmy Weir (R.I.P.) (Raharney) and Jimmy Glynn (Rathwire) Well done, lads!

(Left) Tony Murtagh, Patricia Rogers, Jimmy Weir *(Right)* Jimmy Weir, Tony Murtagh.

Committee

Our committee comprised of Anne Maher (Group Leader) Winnie Daly (Secretary) and Mary Briody (Treasurer) In 2005, Tony Murtagh and Mary Briody visited the children in their hometown of Novozybkov, Western Russia as well as calling to and supporting many orphanages in need.

Sincere Thanks

We wish to take this opportunity to thank everybody who helped us down through the years for their wonderful support, otherwise this great task would not have been possible. Hopefully, we will always remember the children from Chernobyl, in the knowledge that they will never forget the huge generosity of the Killucan/Raharney/Kinnegad people. The Raharney Host Families were (1) Bernard and Helen Murtagh, (2) Gwen (R.I.P.) and Joe Carter, (3) Olive and Nickey Weir.

Tidy Towns

On the front page of the Westmeath Examiner, Saturday, September 20, 1969, the headline reads "Raharney's Great Progress." Detailed in the report is the remarkable improvement that Raharney had made in the Country's Tidy Towns Competition. The Competition honours the tidiest and most attractive cities, towns, and villages in the Republic of Ireland. In that year's Competition, the little village of Raharney had improved in position by no less than forty marks, only eleven marks behind the overall winner. The report states that when a search is made for a village making most progress, in comparison to the previous year, Raharney stands well clear.

Joe Mullen - Chairperson, Tidy Towns Committee.

Among the comments from the judges, it is noted that "there is a complete absence of litter" while "all the properties on the village are well maintained and some gardens are quite colourful." Throughout the report what stands out is the Community effort and this is noted as "obvious" and to be congratulated, indeed the scoring for effort involved was 33/35. One of the recommendations for the village moving forward was to avoid over-elaboration and fussiness. The advice offered was "when in doubt, simplicity is always best." The overall theme of the report was that Raharney certainly deserved the reward. Well done! Raharney!

George Flanagan

George lived opposite Webb's shop. He was both carpenter and undertaker. His speciality was making bog barrows, vitally necessary in the area and used by almost every family. He also mended wooden implements used by farmers locally. Over many years families called on him to organise funerals for their deceased relatives. His workshop was a building at the side of the house beside where the Filling Station used to be. A coffin stood in the workshop window. He also kept a few animals in the cow park on the Craddenstown Road.

© *Annette Farrell*

Raharney Gun Club

In March 2006, a group of local hunting and shooting enthusiasts got together and it was decided to form a Gun Club in the area. A meeting was held in McHugh's Lounge and at this gathering the Gun Club came into being. The committee formed on the night were:

Chairman: Matthew Mullen
Vice Chairperson: Noel Greville
Secretary: Padraig Duggan
Treasurer: Sean Michael Flanagan

Also in attendance were : Jim Glynn, Paul Dunne, Raymond Mullen, Pat Mullen, Tommy Farrell, Derek McKeogh, Gene Shaw, Melvin Greville, Nick Weir and Fergus Grogan.

The Club is quite active and has matured favourably over the years always trying to undertake a new challenge annually.It started off with one pheasant pen and under the guidances of Gene Shaw a former game keeper, hugely increased the pheasant population in the area. This year 250 pheasants were released. The Club undertook to hatch their own pheasants in the last number of years with the purchase of an incubator and a hatching unit. This has proven to work very well. Also this year the Club planted game crop for the first time and it is hoped to increase this activity in the future. The Club also started a wild duck release program and released ducks into Shay Murtagh's lake and into Brendan Farrelly's Quarry so the duck population in the area has increased overall. It is hoped to form another duck pond in the coming year.

Conservation:
Vermin control is a very important issue for the Club with members helping out farmers trapping especially during lambing time, and they try to purchase some new vermin trapping-equipment yearly. There are currently over thirty feeders out in the area which helps to nurture the birds over the winter with numbers increasing yearly. Regarding conservation needs, the vermin control helps protect the curlew, buzzards and other species in the area. The Club has a plan to build a number of barn owl boxes and in this way to protect the owl population from decline.

Clay Shooting:
During the first few years a number of clay traps were purchased by the Club. This has taken a back seaat over the last few years but it is hoped to get this activity up and running again in the near future for everyone interested in clay pidgeon shooting it's a thrilling sport.

Fund Raising:
A Christmas Raffle is run every year also a pub quiz. Over the last two years we had a bonus ball on the Lotto every week which proved a great success. Without local support we could not keep the Club afloat. It was very easy to form a Club but without the support of the local farmers the Club could not exist. Thank you to everyone for your continuted help and co-operation. Insurance for the Club is with the National Regional Game Council Inurance, over the past sixteen years. The number of members to date is over thirty.

This is a great local Club and congratulations to all involved.

© Noel Greville

The Bog Body

In March 2003, a well-preserved body was accidently found by peat cutters in Clonycavan Bog, Ballivor, Co. Meath. Only the human remains of the man's head and torso are preserved. The forearms, hands and lower abdomen are missing. This adult man was discovered in a modern peat harvesting machine which was more than likely responsible for the dismembering of the lower part of his body.

Bog bodies are not unique in Ireland. However, a team comprising of pathologists, radiographers, police detectives, anatomists, conservators and archaeologists carried out their investigations claiming that this Bog Body stumbled across in the Clonycavan Bog had been brutally murdered over 2,300 years ago. He was killed by a series of blows to the head and chest from a heavy edged weapon, presumably an axe. He was in his early twenties. Theories concerning the frightening manner of his gruesome death vary. A nearby hill that could have-been used for his kingship ceremonies, lead us to believe that he was probably a victim of a ritual sacrifice of some type or other to the pagan gods. He was also disemboweled which was a horrific means of torturing and traumatizing him. The bog became a dumping ground.

He soon became known as the Clonycavan Man, and is one of the main bog bodies discovered in Ireland. These bog bodies are generally remarkably well-preserved due to the conditions beneath the peat terrain. The particular chemistry of bog conditions prevents decay and mummifies human flesh.

After highly detailed forensic examinations it was discovered that the Clonycavan Man was from the Iron Age Period. Radio-carbon investigation determined his death to be between 392 BC and 201 BC. More scientific studies and advanced technology showed that he had a squashed nose, crooked teeth and a thin beard. He was a small man, measuring a modest 5 feet and 5 and ½ inches (1.68 cm) in height and had a distinctive hairstyle spiked so that the hair stood on top, probably a way to make him look taller. He used a gel made from vegetable plant oil mixed with a resin. After testing the resin, investigators claimed it originated from a pine tree nut not native to Ireland, but from a tree only grown in Spain and Southern France. Other tests on his hair showed that his diet was rich in protein in the months leading up to his death which indicates a degree of wealth.

Also in 2003, there was a double find, so to speak. A further male Bog Body was unearthed only 25 miles away. (40 km) The Old Croghan Man in Old Croghan, Co. Offaly.

Another famous Bog Body in Denmark, the Tullund Man became the subject of a poem by Irish Nobel Laureate Seamus Heaney who saw in him the spitting image of his great uncle Hughie. Among the Tullund Man's belongings was a cord tied around his neck, which indicates he was most likely a victim of hangling.

Despite the brutal nature of his death he had an eerily peaceful facial expression. These include punishment for breaking ancient codes of honour. However, regardless of the manner of how these bog bodies died, they are still a human connection to our ancestors. May they all rest in peace.

© Anne Maher

Coakley's Band

There is a heart-warming story about the great sense of loyalty and goodwill that existed between the Coakleys of Raharney and the Coakleys of Derrymore.

When John Coakley of Derrymore married Mary O'Neill in 1910, their close-knit cousins in Raharney crossed over the River Deel every day to help build a house to welcome his new bride. It was quite a journey and while it was lovely being outdoors in the warm summer weather, not so when the bitter cold winter months poured down on them stretching into eternity. Nothing however, would interrupt the loyalty of a job started in need of completion.

Returning home late one evening to Raharney, one of the Coakleys stumbled into the River Deel and had to wriggle his way out. Later it was revealed that he got pneumonia and passed away. Ar dheis De go raibh a hanam!

However, the Coakleys of Derrymore grew up and became famous for their music. They formed the Carolina Cheile Band and achieved great acclaim. Des Briody, formally of Shannon

Coakley's Carolina Showband:
(Back L-R) Philip Lynch, Paddy Coakley, Bernie Coakley, (unknown).
(Front L-R) Billy Geoghegan, Michael Coakley, Richard McEvoy.

Insulations, Killucan, tells me, he was once their Band Manager. He remembers organizing them to play in a Carnival in Co. Roscommon. A giant marquee was erected early one April Sunday night in the 1960's. At that time, there was no music played in halls or anywhere else for that matter during Lent.

No sooner had the Coakleys plugged in their equipment than the lights dimmed and distinguished altogether. The ESB (Electricity Supply Board) was called but there was no quick fix. For fear of unsettling the crowd, as most people travelled miles to get there, the Band got the thumbs up to keep playing as in those days the theory was 'The Show must go on.' At first they played the saxaphone, trumpet and drums. Philip Lynch of San Giovanni Guest House, Joristown, Raharney sang his heart out. He toured the countryside with the Band but didn't play an instrument. He was extremely talented and had a powerful voice. There was a throng of approximately one thousand people in the marquee that night. Gaeity was enhanced when the lights blazed again, then dimmed accordingly.

Music has always played an important role in the social life of the countryside, not to mention it's economic growth. Joe Dolan often cycled from Mullingar to join the Coakleys in Derrymore playing music where the locals gathered to dance on the kitchen flagstone floors. So it seems by all accounts that the Coakley's Carolina Cheile Band always struck a popular cord wherever they went.

© Anne Maher

Five Generations

(Left)	**Demelza Nugent**	(Grandmother)
(Back)	**Mary Maguire**	(Great Grandmother)
(Front)	**Maureen Donoghue**	(Great Great Grandmother)
(Right)	**Kayleigh Nugent**	(Mother)
(Baby)	**Aoibhínn Middleton**	(Baby)

The Grangemore Estate

The name Grangemore House evokes memories of school days, in the late 1940's when we would take the long way home, down the long avenue to visit the big house. The purpose of our visit was to get loads of the beautiful apples, that grew in the two orchards, one with high stone walls all round and the other a more recently planted orchard. We never attempted to enter the orchards to rob apples, why I do not know, maybe we had lots of respect for Mrs. O'Brien.

When we arrived up at the big hall door which to us seemed be twelve-feet high, we knocked loudly. The door was soon opened by Mrs. O 'Brien, a very pleasant and charming woman who invited us into a large room off the entrance hall where there were loads of apples and she told us to take as much as we wished which we did, filling our bags and pockets.

It was said that Mrs. O'Brien was a member of Cumann na mBan (An Irish Republican Women's Paramilitary Organization formed in Dublin on 2 April 1914) in the War of Independence. If this were true it would be in complete contrast with the previous owners of Grangemore, the Magans, and Briscoes, who would be staunch Unionists. Mrs. O'Brien was also believed to be an aunt of the late Justin Graham who taught in Killucan Vocational School in later years and played hurling with Raharney, and Westmeath.

Gerry Foley a relation stayed with the O'Brien's at that time. He was an Agricultural Adviser in Co. Meath and had a baby Ford car, one of the few cars in the parish. He used drive them all to Mass in Raharney on a Sunday. He later became an extremely popular Chief Agricultural Officer in Co. Meath and married Rita Quirke from Clondalee in 1952 and lived near Trim.

After the Land Commission had divided up the Grangemore lands in about 1914, the House and farmyards and remaining lands of 146 acres were advertised in the Westmeath Examiner for sale by auction in 1920. Its presumed it was purchased by Rory O'Brien who lived and farmed there until the early 1950's when Grangemore was again sold.

I remember the O' Brien auction of furniture and farm equipment clearly because of one event. When the sale of a nice armchair that Luke Nolan, a wealthy farmer from Derrymore was sitting on, it sparked off a bit of a bidding war between Luke Nolan and John Guiney a brother of Dennis Guiney's who owned Cleary's Store in Dublin, another wealthy man who owned Corbetstown House and Farm. Nolan who was already sitting on the chair became determined that Guiney was not going to buy it. A sort of a bidding war began between Nolan and Guiney, encouraged by a few onlookers. Nolan finally got the chair but at a high price.

Around this time Grangemore House and remaining lands were bought and sold a few times. A Mr. Jones purchased and farmed there for a few years. Mr. Christopher Murtagh a local man also bought Grangemore, and also farmed there for a few years. The big house was demolished, and a demolition auction was held on Sat 25th March 1958. The auctioneer was Edward J King, Killucan. The amount of material advertised in the Westmeath Examiner gives some idea of the scale and size of the house. Thousands of large blue banger slates, 10,000 ft. of floorboards 5000 ft. of pitched pine and yellow pine joists, 2000 ft. of rafters, hundreds of sash windows, hundreds of doors, many marble fireplaces, window shutters, and many miscellaneous items. No doubt there were many local houses and out offices in the area that were refurbished with some of this material.

The ruins of Grangemore House now stands today as a monument to the past, which was good for the landlords of the eighteen and nineteen centuries who built it, and lived there with great wealth, with everything they wished for. Not so for most of the very poor locals over the centuries of years, that suffered greatly during the famine and had very hard times, with high numbers of child mortality rates, living in hovels.

|Image: Arc Studios|

Previous History and Owners of Grangemore Estate

Grangemore House was built by John Fetherson in 1812. It was a three-storey house of the late Georgian style with thirteen bedrooms at an estimated cost then of £10,000. It's said locally that headstones from Cilaheen a nearby field where unbaptised babies were supposed to be buried, that their gravestones were used in the foundations, there is no evidence to back this up, and will only ever become known if the house is fully demolished.

John Fetherston died 29th June1829. His nephew and executor Edward Briscoe took over the Grangemore Estate and House, fully furnished. The new owner's father Edward John Briscoe 1790/1850 had married Frances, the daughter of Thomas Federstonhaugh of Bracklyn Castle. Despite his family experience of living in Ireland, Edwards tenure of Grangemore was fraught with some difficulties. He married Hester Rynd daughter of James Rynd of Derryvolon, Co Fermanagh and Ryndville Co Meath. Edwards elder brother William Thomas Briscoe of Riverdale 1792 -1854 had married Hester's elder sister Maria Elizabeth in 1818. In 1833 Edward served as High Sheriff of Westmeath. He was shot at through a hole in a hedge when riding up the avenue one evening with his brother James.

During the famine of 1845/50, it is said he was not very generous to the poor and had a constable named Robinson guarding a field of turnips that the hungry people were stealing at night. When Briscoe would retire to bed, Robinson himself a parent with children found sympathy with the people. He would fire a shot from a blunderbuss. Mr. Briscoe thought that was to scare the people away, however Robinson had told them it was safe to come onto the land when he fired the shot as Briscoe was in bed. Edward Briscoe was a great supporter of hare coursing and a keen supporter of Westmeath fox hunting. He was also a noted breeder of prize oxen.

Augusta Elizebeth Magan - Owner Grangemore

When Magan's became owners of Grangemore House sometime around 1870, they were already an extremely wealthy family.

William Henry Magan's marriage to Elizabeth Georgina Loftus of Killyon Manor, Co. Meath brought together great wealth, both having several mansions and 20,000 acres of land in many counties. They had two children but by the time they passed away, their son William Henry Magan M.P. had died of drink and debauchery at 42 years of age, so the family fortune passed on to his sister the once beautiful Augusta Elizabeth Magan.

Augusta Elizabeth Magan who had a some years earlier at 19 years old had been jilted on her wedding day by Captain Richard Bernard from Bernard Castle now known as (Kinnity Castle) whom she loved very much, he didn't show up and went on to marry a widow.

Miss Magan found this difficult to come to terms with and became a sort of a recluse living a life of solitude. When she died on the 26th of October 1905 aged seventy-three, she wished to be laid out in her wedding dress. After her funeral when they opened 77, St Stephens Green, Dublin, her great Georgian Mansion, they found a display of the wedding banquet still spread out for the wedding guests, a banquet that never took place.

She had started buying stuff that she did not need and became a compulsive shopper filling her houses with all sorts of goods, some valuable some not so. After Captain Bernard's death in 1877 his remains were wheeled along Mullingar Railway station on route to his burial. Augusta acquired the trolly that was used and kept it her room until she died in 1905. The Author Charles Dickens visited Dublin in 1858 and heard of Miss Magan's sad tragedy. It is said that he based the character of Miss Havisham of 'Great Expectations' which was published in 1861 on her story'

The Land Commission and Grangemore

The Irish land Commission was set up in 1881 under British rule, as a result of agitation by tenant organizations, the National land League and political pressure.

Under many land acts it helped set fair rents for tenants. Over time it developed into an agency to help tenants purchase their holding from their landlords by providing the finance and administration required. The Land commission also under the Wyndham Act of 1903 undertook the breaking up of large estates and dividing up the land among the local farmers subsidized by the state.

In 1903, facilitated by the Land Commission most small holders who were tenants of Lord Longford who was landlord of all the lands at Craddenstown, including Ballinhee, purchased their holdings. Irish farmers could now buy their land with finance provided by government at an interest rate of 3% over 30 years or until the advance was fully cleared.

Question in U.K. Parliament -
U.K.Parliament 1914: Question to Chief Secretary.

"

On the 29th of April 1914, in reply to a question by Mr. Ginnell, M.P. for Westmeath who asked the Chief Secretary the nature of the Estate Commissioner's in what offers they had received for Grangemore Mansion on the Topping and Magan Estate, with little or no land attached for the purpose of an Institution, or the entire of untenanted land on the estate; the number of congested and landless applicants for portions of it; and, having regard to the need to the distribution of all land on the estate. Amid complaints made of the Commissioner making presents of large farms with mansions to people never contemplated under the act. If he will say what other offers applications the commissioners have received for the Mansion, with or without land, and how they intend to dispose of the untenanted land on this Estate

"

Reply from Chief Secretary:

"

This estate which has recently been acquired by the Estate Commissioners under section 6 of the land Act,1903, comprises of 1,900 acres of untenanted land. When, as in this case, there is a large Mansion house on the lands. It is the practice of the Commissioners to preserve such Mansion House, and to sell it with such lands that will preserve its amenities. The Commissioners have let the Mansion House and some 120 acres of the adjoining lands, including plantations to the Rev. B.M. Ryan at a yearly rent of £100 with option to purchase. He intends to use it as a training institute for the blind. The Commissioners are not yet able to state how many of the applications for allotments of untenanted land fall within the classes indicated by the Honourable Member. All applications received are with the inspector who is at present framing a scheme for allotment.' END OF REPLY.

"

By 1920 The Rev B.M. Ryan had not taken up his option to purchase, Grangemore House and lands, and no Institute for the blind came about. Dividing up the land among local small farmers who only had exceedingly small holdings in most cases poor boggy land commenced about this time, and by the end of 1914 most allocations of Grangemore land was complete.

To get an allocation of good land was a great boost to their income and particularly to become owner of their farm meant a great deal. This was the first time ever in our history that a tenant could own his land, provided he keep up the payments which was due on 1st June and the 1st Dec. each year. It certainly was not free and was hard to pay at times. Additional land to local farmers who were very much in need of increasing the size of their holdings was a big help in improving their livelihoods. The cost to purchase by the commissioners based on the advance made was approx. £23 per acre plus 3 % interest. Re-payments by the farmer were half-yearly over 30 years or until the advance was paid in full.

© Shay Callaghan

Dramatic Fire Rescue of 88 Year Old Woman

 ## Comairle na Mire Saile

Thursday, 3 June, 2004 • Issue No. 1695

Dramatic fire rescue of 88 years old woman

Neighbour risks life to save octogenarian

A man, who is a neighbour and an employee of an 88 years old widow, rushed into her blazing home of Tuesday morning of this week, June 1st 2004, to rescue the elderly lady who was in bed at the time, as fire raged through part of the house and threatened her life.

As fire engulfed the bungalow of Mrs Doris Gibson, Grangebeg, Raharney, her neighbour and employee, Peter Farrelly, who was some distance off, noticed smoke coming from the house. He rushed to the scene and tried to gain entrance through the rear of the house but was beaten back by the smoke. He rushed to the front of the bungalow and gained entry through the front door, for which he had a key. He rescued Mrs. Gibson from her bed as the flames began to spread through the building.

Other neighbours, John and Mattie Gartland and Peter's son, James were quickly on the scene and assisted Peter in bringing the elderly lady to safety.

Describing what happened, Peter said that he was out on the road at about 7.00am and he looked across towards Gibsons.

"It would be normally about 8.00am when I would get in to work. I would look at the sheep and cattle and then go to the house. Someone was definitely praying for her (Mrs. Gibson), that's all I can say," added Peter.

"I saw smoke and I knew that there should not have been smoke. I was about 500 or 600 yards from the house, and the smoke was blowing away from it at this time."

"When I got to the house, there was smoke billowing out from the top of the door and from the windows. I couldn't get in through the back because of the smoke and the heat. I rushed to the front of the house. I have a key and I let myself in, and I went to find Mrs. Gibson, who was in bed. I brought her out.

"When I went in, I didn't have my mobile phone and I went to get into the kitchen where Mrs. Gibson's phone was, but when I opened the cross door in the hallway going to the kitchen, the smoke and the flames beat me back. The roof of the house was on fire then. I rushed back and got Mrs. Gibson out, and we put her in a van until the ambulance came and took her to hospital," Peter added.

TWENTY YEARS

He said that he has been working for Mrs. Gibson for twenty years and he looks after the stock, sheep and cattle. Her husband, Johnny died over 30 years ago and the couple have no family.

He added that Mrs. Gibson was very concerned and upset about the welfare of her collie dog, "Jill".

"The dog used to stay in the house with her at night. I suppose she was a protection for her in case of anyone trying to get into the house," added Peter.

Thankfully, Mrs. Gibson's dog escaped from the fire.

As Mrs. Gibson was being removed from the house, Mullingar Fire Service was being alerted about the outbreak by Peter Farrelly's wife, Margaret.

Two units of Mullingar Fire service were quickly on the scene, arriving at 7.30pm, but by that stage the fire had got into the roof, which collapsed, and the house was completely gutted.

Gardai from Mullingar also arrived on the scene and a forensic examination took place.

SHOCK AFTERWARDS

Recalling the incident afterwards, Peter said that when he later thought about the fire, he got a fright, but at the time all he was conscious of was Mrs. Gibson being in the house and the only thing he wanted to do was to get her out safely.

"When I got to the back door and saw the smoke billowing out I knew that it was serious. I just rushed round to the front and got in and got her out. She was my only thought at the time. I didn't think of the danger, it didn't enter my head. I knew that there was a person in the house and that the fire was very bad and if I didn't get her out.......

"At the time you don't realise the danger, not until it is all over and you have time to think back. The house just went up in minutes when the roof collapsed."

"Mrs. Gibson was most concerned about her dog "Jill" but she is all right."

He said that the house occupant was completely unaware that the house was on fire.

"She said that she heard some crackling, but she didn't know what it was", added Peter.

It is understood that Mrs. Gibson was uninjured, but she was detained in the Midland Regional Hospital at Mullingar for observation.

A spokesperson from Mullingar Fire service confirmed that they had been called to the Raharney fire and arrived at 7.30 am.

Peter Farrelly was awarded a Silver Medal and a Certificate of Bravery

Congo 1960

The United Nations embarked on the biggest mission in history to the then Belgian Congo in 1960, with 20,000 soldiers from thirty countries. At the centre of the storm were 155 soldiers of the A Company, the 33rd Battalion of the Irish Army.

The eyes of the world were on Katanga, a fabulously wealthy breakaway province, controlled by white European colonists mercenaries and giant mining companies. The notorious Niemba Ambush took place on 8th. November 1960, when an Irish Army patrol in Congo-Leopoldville was ambushed.

Pierce Gilbride

Pierce Gilbride was born in Robinstown, Navan, Co. Meath in 1941 and joined the Army at the age of fifteen, having obtained a three year apprenticeship in woodwork and carpentry in Devoy Barracks, Naas, Co. Kildare. From there he served in Custume Barracks, Athlone, Co. Westmeath. During this time he met his future wife Teresa, a native of Loughrea in 1960 when he was nineteen years old and she was eighteen years old.

On the 17th August, 1960, Pierce was deployed with the 33rd Infantry Battalion for a six months tour of duty to the Congo, Africa, as part of the U.N. Peacekeeping Mission there. (ONUC) A few months later, on Tuesday, 8th November, members of the 33rd Inf. Battalion suffered what still remains the greatest tragedy ever to befall the Irish Army, with nine members of an eleven-man patrol killed, four of them close personal friends of Pierce Gilbride.

Day Before the Ambush

Poignantly, on Monday, 7th November, the day before the tragic Niemba Ambush, Pte. Pierce Gilbride was a member of the patrol working on the road to Niemba. The patrol was ordered back to its headquarters after the officer in charge became uneasy about the situation and feared for the safety of his men. Had they not returned to base, they would all probably have been killed.

Nine Killed

On the 8th November, the eleven-man section from the 33rd Battalion arrived at the bridge over the Luweyeye River. They were forced to leave their vehicles when they came upon a road blockade. While concentrating on clearing the roadblocks around NIEMBA, they encountered dozens of Baluba tribesmen armed with bows, poison-tipped arrows, spears, clubs and some guns. While the Irish troops were there to protect them, the Baluba tribesmen mistook them for the Katangan mercenaries. The section leader, Lt. Kevin Gleeson, a military engineer, advanced unarmed, with his platoon sergeant, Hugh Gaynor. He greeted them peacefully, but were met with a barrage of poison-tipped arrows. Lt. Gleeson and Sgt. Gaynor were immediately overtaken and killed. The surprised Irish soldiers, who had not been deployed in a defensive formation, retreated behind trees on either side of the road and opened fire.

Then more Balubas advanced from all directions from behind the bushes and high grasses nearby. The Irish were cut off from their vehicles. They were completely overrun and in hand-to-hand fighting, most of the Irish troops were killed. The survivors re-grouped but were surrounded. All but three were annihilated. One of them escaped, Anthony Browne and sought help in a nearby village but instead he was mobbed and beaten to death. His body was recovered two years later. The two surviving soldiers managed to conceal themselves and were found by other members of the 33rd Battalion, including Pte. Pierce Gilbride, still a teenager, the following day.

Pierce Gilbride was part of the recovery team which searched for the bodies of the Irish soldiers afterwards, something he was never able to speak about for the rest of his life. Pierce was promoted to Corporal in 1961 and spent eight years in the Army.

He lived in Riverdale, Raharney, Co. Westmeath where his wife Teresa still lives. He worked for several years with Dermot Solon, then with Shay Murtagh Precast, Raharney. Pierce and Teresa married in 1965, and have two children, Fiona Gilbride (Cully) and Martin Gilbride.

U.N. Veterans to Honour Congo Survivors

On Sunday, 3rd September 2017, there was a large attendance at a Mass in St. Joseph's Church, Rathwire, Killucan, Co. Westmeath celebrated by Fr. Mark English, and later in the nearby St. Joseph's Cemetery, to honour Pierce Gilbride, a survivor of the United Nations Peacekeeping Service in the Congo, Africa. Fr. English referred to the dedicated service of so many members of our Defence Forces, especially those listed on the Military Memorial in front of the altar in the cemetery at Rathwire. Attending were members of Post 20 Mullingar, of the Irish United Nations Veterans' Association (IUNVA) and the Mullingar branch of the Organization of National Ex-Servicemen and Women, together with justifiably proud family members, public representatives serving the former members of the Defence Forces, and members of the public attending the ceremony. The (IUNVA) members were led by Eddie Robinson, Mullingar, the National Chairman of (IUNVA) and by James Reilly, the President of Post 20, Mullingar (IUNVA) while the members of ONE were led by Tom Gunn, Chairman of the Mullingar Branch. Gunn himself, a survivor of the UN service in Congo, who was held as a prisoner for six weeks after the Battle of Jadotville.

Netflix have brought out a film "The Siege of Jadotville" showing how the Irish troops were outmanned and outgunned and had to fight for their lives in the heat of the desert.

Here is a copy of Martin Gilbride's (Son of Pierce) speech at St. Joseph's Cemetery, Rathwire, Co. Westmeath. (3rd September 2017):

Pierce Gilbride.

Good morning everyone. Martin Gilbride is my name. I am here today with my mother Teresa, sister Fiona and our families, also Daddy's brother George.

I will tell you a bit about his life, starting in Robinstown, Navan, where he was born. There were three children in the family. He attended National School in Robinstown, then onto Secondary School in Trim, where in class one day, the Headmaster mentioned to the pupils, if anyone was interested in Army Apprenticeship Courses, there was a three year course starting in Devoy Barracks in Naas. He asked the class to think about it anyhow.

So, with good advice and approval from home, Daddy decided to do the course. He chose to do Woodwork and Carpentry. It was hard to be going away from home I'm sure, as he was only fifteen years old in 1956, but he made a few lifelong friends there.

After completing his apprenticeship, he was to be based in Custume Barracks, Athlone, from where, with other men, he would have to go to different towns around the country for short periods to do some maintenance work. In January 1960, he was working in a town in Galway, a place called Loughrea, where he met my mother and of course it was 'love at first sight.' He was nineteen and she was eighteen.

The romance blossomed, but joy turned to tears when he told her in July that year, that he was going to the Congo – a six month tour of duty with the 33rd Infantry Battalion, and so off they went. In his 1st letter home to my mother, he said the journey was very long, very bumpy and so hot but they eventually arrived to the place where they were to be stationed for six months – a place called Albertville. They went about their duties each day, patrolling in and around the town area. The people were 'friendly enough' he said, 'but a bit distant.' Sometimes, as part of their duties, they would have to travel away from the town, clearing roads from fallen trees, bushes and debris, etc. so that traffic bringing supplies to the town and to the Railway Station could flow freely.

On 7th November 1960, they were working in the Niemba area – work was about to finish for the day when they heard disturbances all around them in the bush. They were told to back away to their transport and go – and they did. Next day was the 8th November, and a new group of men came there to continue on the work from the day before but tragically they were ambushed and killed. Thankfully two soldiers survived, badly injured and traumatized. They were eventually able to relay the story of everything that happened. As it turned out, my father was part of the recovery team, sent out to search for them and bring them back. An experience he said would be with him for ever and that he knew a few of them fairly well. May they rest in peace! On the day the bodies were to be sent home to Ireland for their funerals, he said that there was a Mass very early in the morning at the Airport. They all had to be up at 4.00am and after a Military Ceremony with heavy hearts, the coffins were put on the plane for home. From then on he said all he could think of was seeing the 'Green Fields of Ireland' again but they would have to wait two more months for that.

To finish now, everything I have told you today he put in letters sent home to my mother, all of which she has today in perfect condition – 57 years later. Daddy was in the army for eight years. He was promoted to Corporal in 1961, got married to the Galway Girl in 1965, spent all his life with her and their children in Raharney, Co. Westmeath.

Up at the crack of dawn everyday for work, after his usual breakfast of shredded wheat and tomato juice – he would be off with his lunchbox under his arm until July, 2008, the Lord called him.

Thank you,
Martin Gilbride

Riverdale House

Riverdale House, Raharney

Riverdale House, Raharney was built by the Briscoe family in about 1760. The Briscoes came from the North Midlands of England and resided at Screggan, Tullamore from 1570.

William Briscoe married Irene Nugent of Derrymore in 1761, and they came to live at Riverdale House. His son, Edward, married Frances Fetherston of Bracklyn, and inherited Riverdale in 1781. Edward's son , William ,born 1792, inherited Riverdale in, or ,about 1825.

His son, Edward,born 1829, married Anna Rebecca Smith,Marriott in 1852, and she died at Riverdale in about 1932, aged 102 years. Their only son, Edward, lived on at Riverdale for about six years, and then went back to live at Screggan, Tullamore.

The house was sold to Charles Smith, who lived there for a few years, when, due to his failure to keep the chimneys properly swept, a fire began and the house burned down. Only the walls were left standing. The estate with the ruined house was sold to a Mr. Millmoe, who lived in the ruins for a few years until it was eventually bought by M.D. Solon, Esq. From Galway.

He rebuilt the house as nearly as he could to the plan of the original house, and lived there until early 1996, when the entire estate was sold to Mr. Shay Murtagh.

It appears that the Briscoes never did anything of note, but lived quietly at Riverdale, farming and living a life of leisure. The last Edward did go to America for about seven years, and lived on a ranch in the Wild West. His mother, Anna, at that time 97 years, went out to America to stay with him. She came home two years later,in time to celebrate her 100th birthday at Riverdale, and apart from being deaf,she kept all her faculties and was an extremely lively old lady.

Shay Murtagh

I was born in 1946. I was the eldest of nine children. We lived in Joristown (Rodney's Hill). I remember the ESB coming in 1952. I went to school in Raharney in St. Mary's National School, the old school out the Wardenstown Road. I always call it U.C.R, University College Raharney. When I was 12 years of age, I remember Mr. Dinneen calling to the house asking my mother to send me to vocational school. I spent about one or two years there. My father was a Miller, working in Thomastown Mill. He was there for 23 years. There was never anything to do in the mill during the summer, so we spent the summers in the bog. We cut turf for sale and we also worked in Bord na Móna. At that time, there would be 200 people working in the bog.

When I was 15, I asked Dermot Solon for a job. He said he'd give me an apprenticeship and I started the following Monday. I was earning 11 pence per hour. At that time, there were 240 pence in a pound and I made 2 pound per week. There were 6 people working at concrete in Riverdale. The following year, I was making 1 shilling and 3 pence per hour. Tommy Lynam was the carpenter and Tom Shanahan was the foreman.

My first job away from the Riverdale yard was a job for Mr. Wright in Hyde Park, Annascannon, Killucan, Co. Westmeath. I now had a new foreman, Packie McCabe from Cloone, in Co.Leitrim. For the next two years, I worked in various parts of the country. Every now and then, I would go and help Tommy Lynam to build a reservoir. There was a cement strike in 1966 and a builders strike. I went to Sligo to build a small factory for a Mr. Waters. When I had the factory built, I was still working for Riverdale Concrete Products. I decided it was time to do something else. I got a job with McInerneys at Island Bridge, Dublin. I was doing 2nd fixing, hanging doors. We were on piece work. We had 7 shilling and 6 pence per door. I didn't spend much time at that.

I, then, got a job with Bantile Ltd. in Banagher, Co. Offaly. The first job that I was sent to was in Stranorlar, Co. Donegal. The general foreman was Da Eagan. He questioned me about what I had worked at in the past. The building they were putting up was a pre-cast building. He put me setting out, I was home and dry. I spent the next two years with that company working all over Ireland. In 1968, Tommy Lynam asked me to build a pre-cast reservoir in Killybegs, Donegal. We agreed on the money between us, that was when I began working for myself.

In 1967, I met my future wife at a dance in Collinstown. She was working in Whelehan's Chemist in Mullingar. She had applied for a job in the Civil Service and in 1968 she began working in the telephone exchange in Exchequer Street, Dublin. I was building reservoirs all over Ireland. We would only see one another on the weekends. In 1970, we started looking for a site to build our home. We wanted to be near Dublin because that was where the work was. I certainly did not see myself travelling all over Ireland once we were married. We bought a half acre site in Enfield, Co. Meath. We received a mortgage from Meath County Council and built the house ourselves. We got married in 1971 and at that time, there was a marriage ban on women working within the civil service. We went to Spain on our honeymoon, our first time on an aeroplane. I was 25 and Doreen was 23.

The Ancient Arms of

Murtagh

[Image: Arc Studios]

The reservoir business was very up and down. Work was never consistent, so I turned to do other things. I was subcontracting for Riverdale Concrete Products, putting up factories and roofing. I did some pre-cast erecting with Galway Concrete and Group Water Works in Dublin. I was still working all over Ireland. I would be away Monday to Friday. In 1972, we rented a flat in Milford in Donegal for three months as I had a lot of work in that area.

The 70's in Ireland were a bad time. Interest rates were at 19%. There was a bank strike. Life was not easy. My brother, Ber, joined us in 1973 and stayed with us until he died in 2007. Jim Reilly joined us in 1975 and is still with us as I write today. In 1976, we bought two sites in Ballinla, Killucan from a builder that was getting out of the building trade. One house had the timber on the roof. We sold our house in Enfield and we moved to Ballinla, Killucan. When we would finish a job down the country, we came back to Ballinla to build our second home. All the lads we had at the time did not enjoy building the house. So in 1977, I saw precast moulds for sale in Galway and I bought them for £2,150. I brought them home in a trailer I was pulling with my car. My father gave me a half an acre site at the back of our home in Joristown. This was the beginning of manufacturing precast. Over the next few years, we bought small bits of land from our neighbours in Joristown and there was always about six people working at the precast manufacturing.

In 1978, Galway Concrete went into liquidation. Riverdale Concrete went into liquidation in 1980. We were owed £14,000 for labour. This was a very difficult time in Ireland, the banks were a disaster. I have many letters on file where they have refused to loan me money, but that story would fill a book of its own. Irish Cement would not give us cement, we had to buy through an agent. In 1982, I was approached by a Dr. Fred Hogg, who had only arrived in Joristown. After a long discussion, he was looking for me to 'front' him to buy Riverdale Concrete from the liquidator. He had a company in Northern Ireland, called Macrete, He was going to use Riverdale as storage for the Irish market. I told him that I would have to think about it. Doreen and I discussed what to do and decided that I should head back to the banks. There was fifteen acres on the site in Riverdale with no raw materials. I approached a businessman in Dublin to purchase the factory in Riverdale but he looked at me and said 'Shay, why would I buy a bog?' I went back to the banks and gave them the deeds for our home and for Joristown. They allowed me to borrow £80,000. We were now owners of Riverdale Concrete Products in liquidation. Now the real work started.

Dermot Solon owned the farm next to the factory. He was selling sand and stone. He was giving me lots of problems. I was buying sand and aggregate from different suppliers in the area. So, after about a year he approached me to buy same from him, which I did. In the mid 80's, you were like a beggar man trying to get money. I designed a new reservoir panel to meet the B.S standards. I got Eolas to check the design and get them to put their stamp on it. We were working for every County Council in Ireland. At this time, you knew your money was guaranteed, but unfortunately you never knew when you would get paid. In 1985, we priced the sewage scheme in Killucan. We got the contract. There were a few more contracts like that.

In 1985, we moved the precast manufacturing in Joristown to Riverdale. In 1990, Ireland was starting to pick up again. Work was getting better and it was easier to get paid. In the early 90's, we were manufacturing reservoirs (which we saw as our bread and butter), bridge beams, factory frames, concrete blocks and some specials for clients. In 1988, we put in a new batching system for concrete at a cost of £250,000. We started making ready mix concrete.

In 1995, Dermot Solon was trying to sell the farm and house next door to our factory. After prolonged negotiations, we bought the house and farm which was on 225 acres. That was in 1996. We sold our house in Ballinla and moved into the house in Riverdale in 1998. I still live there today. Dermot Solon had been selling sand since the 1950's, but he was digging holes everywhere on the farm. We bought an old dragline and were digging everything out. We had to buy screeners etc. We had taken out a lease, in 1993, on Paddy Cooney's pit in Annascannon. We were paying Paddy by the ton for everything we took out of the pit. In 2002, we decided to move the plant we had in Cooney's pit to Riverdale. Ber was looking after the farm work and Ciarán was working on making bridge beams. Liam McGovern, who started with us in 1984 and is still with us today as a director of the company, priced most of the building work. I would say that the secret to running a successful business is to surround yourself with good people, people you can trust and people you can speak openly with.

In 2003, Ciarán and Ber went to the U.K and bought a dredger to pump out the sand. The year 2000 onward was a very exciting time in Ireland for the construction industry. We invested in new batching plants, cranes and lorries. We were constantly reinvesting in the business. In 2007, Ber died suddenly. This made me stop and think. Business had to go on. While Ber had worked at everything within the company, he had set up the farming division constructing farm buildings. When he had died, we did not have anyone in the company to keep that part of the business going. I went out onto sites myself and finished the jobs we had. I then closed down that part of the business. Doreen had been taking a back seat in the accounts side of the business and Jim Buckley had begun taking over her role.

In 2009, Ciarán went to the U.K and sourced some precast work. We manufactured in Raharney and sent the products to the U.K. In 2010, when I was 64 years of age, I decided to pass on the business to my son Ciarán and my daughter Gillian. It's not easy to hand on what you have spent your life building. I was never one for standing around and thinking about things. The decision was made.

They have grown the business into a multimillion euro company. We have a factory in the U.K with 80 people employed and a design office in Portugal with 25 people in total. We have an excess of 300 employees.

Shay Murtagh Precast

'From Tiny Acorns Great Oaks Grow;' An old proverb which is very appropriate in relation to the growth of Shay Murtagh Precast Concrete Raharney.

This company from very small beginnings, manufacturing small precast products in the 1970's developed into a large international company, suppling large precast concrete products literally across the world. Shay Murtagh and his family over the years have through good planning and hard work achieved great success, creating steady employment, and other spin off benefits to the area. They have also been great supporters of the Community and all sporting organizations.

The residents of Raharney and the local area would be aware of these large trucks loaded with concrete products travelling through the village daily, and I am sure would often wonder where they were going. Perhaps destined for some the of large contracts in Ireland, England, and across Europe or as far away the Antarctic, where Shay Murtagh Precast delivered 1,000 individual precast products for their client BAM a contract to Modernise U.K. Antarctic Research. They could be one of the 160 loads of precast concrete units to be loaded onto the Wagenborg, one of the largest ships to enter Dublin Port, which would have to fit ice breaking equipment before setting out on its long voyage to Baffin Island, Canada one of the most Northern iron ore mines in the World. You may have noticed a truck on its way to Scotland with concrete units for a Shetland Island Contract, or one of the 3,400 loads of precast concrete tunnel segments for the 5.5km connecting East and West London Rail Routes.

Another major contract is London City Airport. If you happen to pass through London city airport, you will be landing on a precast concrete runway, manufactured here in Raharney.

Now in retirement having passed on the responsibility of the company to his son Ciaran and daughter Gillian, he nevertheless continues to inspire others with his enterprising spirit. The death of his wife Doreen, a few years ago was a big blow. However, Shay busies himself with lots of voluntary and charitable projects.

© *Shay Callaghan*

(Left) Great grandfather Andy Murray *(Middle Left)* Grandmother Jenny (Elizabeth) Murray *(Middle Right)* Grandfather Andy. Andrew Murray (Ballinaskeagh) married to Anne Kenny in 1890. His son, also Andrew (Ballinaskeagh), married in Raharney Church on 3rd June 1914 to Anne Gilchrist from Grange Ballynacargy. Andrew died in 1950 and Anne in 1962. They had a family of six - Tess (Raleigh), Nan (Flanagan), Molly (Cashin), Lil (Murtagh), Joe and Andy (Coventry). Lil married Barney Murtagh (Joristown) on 18th April 1945 and they had a family of ten and so the connection of the Murtaghs in Raharney and surrounding areas. Lil died in 1965 and Barney died in 1993.

(Right) Valerie Murtagh 1962-2018 - Valerie was a very loved and respected member of the community of Riverdale, Raharney and further afield. She had a great love for her family and friends and was especially devoted to her parents Mick and Mary. She had a generous and kind nature an a great sense of humour. Her illness did not deter her from achieving her goals and her love of music and art was a reflection of her zest for life and it showed in the many beautiful paintings she created. She faced all of life's challenges with a positive outlook and this was a true inspiration to all who knew her. She was one in a million.

Dermot Solon

In 1952, Dermot Solon bought Riverdale house and farm which was approximately 330 acres. In doing land reclamation on the farm, he discovered the farm was infested with rabbits. As a result, he discovered that there was an extensive bed of sand underneath the farm.

In 1953, he was offered a license for the manufacture of arrow precast units by BSR of Cardiff in Wales. The engineers from Cardiff came to Raharney and checked the sand and it was agreed to set up a factory on the site. This was the beginning of Riverdale Concrete Products. Precast products are very labour intensive. In 1954, the company supplied floor slabs to various sites, the first being the military barracks in Athlone. Around the year 1958, Liam Geoghan, a local tradesman, built a 20,000 gallon circular water tank for a Captain McCarthy in Bracklyn Estate, using arrow units manufactured by Riverdale Concrete Products. When Dermot saw what could be done with arrow units, he formed two more companies; Nolos Farm Buildings and Nolos Reservoirs. He also formed a company called River Securities to sell sand and gravel.

Dermot also purchased a Joinery in Buttevant in Cork and he started to make precast products alongside the joinery. His brother-in-law, Sam Holt, was running the factory. He also purchased a company in Mulhuddart in Dublin called 'Wall Units'. This company manufactured precast wall panels for housing and there were a lot of 'one off' houses built all over Ireland.

In 1981, the group of companies went into liquidation except River Securities Ltd. This company continued trading until 1996. Dermot was also involved in the hotel business; The Glentworth hotel in Limerick, The Greville Arms Hotel in Mullingar and the Portumna Hotel in Portumna, Co. Galway.

In his younger years, he played hurling for Clare and was centre half back in the Railway Cup in 1946, playing with Munster. When he gave up the hurling he took up golf. In 1998, Dermot went into his eternal reward. *Ar dheis de go raibh a anam.*

Mary Harris Organist

Mary Harris was a well-known, long-serving organist in Raharney Church, accompanying the choir at Mass, each Sunday morning.

In reality, no replacement will ever be found for our Mary. She gave us years of enjoyment and amusement. She loved her music. To her, it wasn't a job, it was a passion. She went to college and studied until she attained a music degree and became a Certified Professional Organist. Nothing but the very best for Mary and the congregation of Raharney reaped the benefits.

She crafted the delivery of her music for all types of events, both small and large. Weddings, First Holy Communions, Confirmations, Christmas Carols and all the atmospheric ceremonies around Christmas and Easter, through which she provided us with several memorable events along the way, always exceeding our expectations and bringing us closer into God's presence. Mary was also a long serving member of the Tidy Towns.

I have a feeling that St. Peter has already steered Mary Harris through the Pearly Gates, that she is now in Heaven, laughing out loud, looking down on us all in Raharney with intrigue and curiousity, wondering what we're at.

© Anne Maher

Raharney Apostolic Society

The Raharney Apostolic Society was founded to raise money to provide vestments, chalices, and altar cloths for the Missions. In 1954-1955 members included Mary Flanagan, Margaret Dargan (who crafted altar lace) Nan Grimes, Lil Farrell, Betty Swords, Philomena Anderson, Jenny McManus, and Nan Coakley.

In later years, the Society organised the "Bring and Buy" to raise funds. Ann Brennan, Una Weir and Rosaleen Barry organised this yearly event. There was always help from Kathleen Nolan, Mary Harris, Regina O'Keeffe, and Olive Weir. On the day, Jimmy Weir was the regular, enthusiastic and effective 'Auctioneer.' The event took place in the National School and was well supported, and good fun. Fruit Cakes were guaranteed to bring in quite a few pounds. People also donated potatoes and other vegetables. Donations came in from a multitude of villagers and the surrounding areas. These included jam from Doris Gibson, May Potterton made candles, potatoes from Nicky Weir, Kathy McKeogh sold tickets, just to mention a few. Local families always supported and attended the event, including the Mullen and Mulvaney Families.

The money raised allowed the Apostolic Society to purchase silverware and material. Those involved at that time included Joe Mooney, Olive Green, Olive Weir, Ann Brennan, Una Weir, Camilla Bray, and Nuala Dargan.

The immaculate display on Mission Sunday was always impressive, including hand knitting, ten sets of vestments and altar cloths which no doubt would travel to the far corners of the earth.

© Rosaleen Barry

Matt Gartland

On the 23rd September 2022 and 29th September, we (Anne Maher, Lillie Connaughton, Shay Murtagh, Rita Monaghan) met up with Matt Gartland to record his recollections of Raharney and his involvement in the village. Matt was born on the 22nd September 1930 and had celebrated his 92nd birthday the previous day. His good-humour, wit and intellect were very evident on the day.

Matt was part of his father's business from an early age, and he eventually took over the business in Riverdale, Raharney. His father Jack Gartland had originally started a general carpentry business. In the *Gartland Family History records Jack and the Raharney branch of the Gartland family is described as follows: -*'Jack Gartland, casket and hurley maker, formerly a coach builder and contractor, lives with his wife in a neat house in Raharney, Westmeath. A modest man, he has prospered. Sons Matthew and Desmond use the plant, which is a few hundred yards down the road and across it. House and plant are located in the countryside. Sean Gartland, another son, is the salesman. Daughter of the manufacturer is Christie, Mrs. Patrick Turley, who lives at 10 Dalton Place, Salt Hill, Galway. Patrick is engaged in the building business. Another daughter is Mrs. Nuala McKinley, wife of a scientist. The couple reside in San Raphael, California. Mary the third daughter, is married and living near Raharney.' Matt recalled that his Dad was a foreman in Dublin prior to and at the start of WW2 (The Emergency). All during the war years their home had an electric wind charger which generated electricity for their home in Raharney. His father came home every weekend to check the generator and ensure the supply of electricity for the home.

Jack got caught up in the North Strand Bombing which occurred on the night of the 30th/31st May 1941, when four high explosive bombs were dropped over Dublin's North Strand area by German aircraft. The impact resulted in the death of twenty-eight people. Over ninety people suffered injuries, and the bomb also caused the destruction of three hundred houses. Fortunately, Jack anticipated the 3rd bomb, from the whistling down from the plane, and he left his house which was situated at the rear of the Five Lamps. His only injury was dust in his eyes. Following this, he returned to Raharney and did not go back to Dublin.

During this period (1940's) while working in Dublin, Jack spotted an opening in the market for charcoal and started the production of charcoal in Raharney. The pit where he worked is still in Gibson's field. The thinning of the hawthorn tree was then converted into charcoal. The charcoal was at that time brought by horse and dray to the Hill of Down for transportation to Dublin by Dublin Docks. Matt's father now supplied charcoal for steam lorries belonging to the company that he had previously worked for 'The Dublin Glass and Paint Company.'

Their business also included the shoeing and making of wheels for carts and drays. This process began with a fire made from an ass-load of turf. The heat when ready, rendered the iron pliable so that it fit in an iron band around the cartwheel. The cartwheel then made of wood, so the correct skill was required to ensure that while the metal was hot, the wooden wheel did not burn. Matt acquired this skill by imitating his father.

Matt's family moved to Monasterevin, Co. Laois, when he was six years old. He started National School there with the Sisters of Mercy. The family continued to live in Monasterevin for two years, and Matt received his First Holy Communion there. His brother Sean attended the Christian Brothers. On Matt's return to Raharney, he was taught by Master O'Brien who was very kind and generous 'a total gentleman.' He recalled how the master would call children to his window, to share cake with them at lunch time. When Master O'Brien retired a new principal Master Conway was appointed in his place. At about the age of eleven years, Matt attended Killyon National School, for the final part of his formal education. He stayed for one year, as it was a long journey, on a bad bicycle. When he left school, he was hardly able to write his name and spent the next few years with his father in the family business learning his trade.

Matt's first job outside the family business was to assist roofing Riverdale House, Raharney. From there he got a job with Charlie Doyle & Sons, Builders, on a scheme of two-storey houses in Mullingar. Matt was responsible for finishing every house for inspection by the Clerk of Works. Owen Doyle was the owner/engineer. Johnny Mullen was the electrician on the job. Matt, who was 18 years old at that time, acted as foreman. He was paid £6.40 per week which was good money at the time. He also started a correspondence course with a College in England studying Maths, which cost him a lot of money, where they sent you questions, and the student posted back the answers. In 1951, he went to work in Dublin for O'Connor & Bailey, putting on an extension for the Gresham Hotel. The foreman worked with his uncle Jim Gartland at the building of the airport, he used his pull to get Matt into the joinery works in Black Pitts. This meant he could attend night classes twice a week in Bolton Street and he use to walk back to Ballsbridge to John Mooney's B&B. O'Connor & Bailey put him in charge of reinventing a

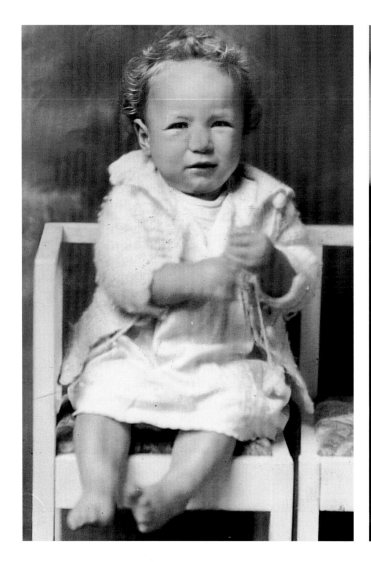

big pub called the Oval Bar which is still there on the corner of Abbey & O'Connell Street, Dublin. In 1954 Matt joined his father doing the woodwork on six houses in Ballivor, Co. Meath. The second week on the job he fell through a ceiling and landed on a concrete block which knocked out four vertebrae of his spine. Matt spent eight months in 'plaster of paris' from his chin to his hips.

The production of hurleys started in c.1950's. Matt recalls driving to the Dock area where The Point Depot now stands. It soon became the distribution place for his hurleys. Lilly Connaughton worked for Matt in the 1960's in the office in the front room of their home when they were building the Bank of Ireland in Enfield. He remembers having the first phone line in the area. A supply of ash trees was originally sourced, from the bottom of Croagh Patrick but later, due to a disease affecting the Irish trees it was necessary to import ash from Europe. Matt was a good hurler and decided to make his own hurley stick and supply them to the local team. He trained two young men from a Rural Care facility in Tuam, to glue the hurley's. They stayed with Mrs. Petite in Raharney. Afterwards both found themselves jobs elsewhere. The business grew from there and expanded into coffin making. Matt was involved with the Raharney Hurling team for years as a player and an avid supporter. Matt's skill and experience on the hurling pitch was invaluable in his production and design of hurley sticks.

Matt, his brother the late Sean Gartland and the late Jimmy Rooney, having finished building The Bank of Ireland Building in Killucan and Enfield started a job for Joe Coyne in Kilcock, converting his butcher's shop to a Hardware Merchants. At this time (1964) the electricity was being installed in the plant in Raharney and while everything was under control a fire started, due to an electrical fault and everything was lost including hurls, coffins, machinery, and accounts. Matt was working in Kilcock at that time and only his father was at home to witness the devastation.

Hockey sticks were being manufactured in the plant in the early seventies using waste material from the hurleys. Dr. DeCourcy Wheeler introduced the hockey sticks to a player and over a period of two years the English hockey team used Matt's hockey sticks. Enterprise Ireland got an inquiry from the Dunlop Manufacturing Company to sell the hockey sticks worldwide. John Sisk built the factory on a half-acre site (original homeplace), and they went into production. Unfortunately, in 1974 with five thousand hockey sticks ready for the German market a fire started and everything was burned. Matt had fourteen men working that day and as he was trying to put out the fire, he burnt his hands very badly. He was six months in hospital. It took him five years to gain back full mobility.

In 1953 Matt built his present home. He purchased .5 acre from Thomas O'Keeffe. He cut down four big ash trees on the edge of the road and opened the site. It was done with a spade and shovel crosscut. After the second fire he built his present factory beside his home. In 1970 Rivdal Enterprises Ltd was formed. The company manufactures coffin panels for the burial and casket industry. Matt was part of that business from a young age. In the early years coffins, were supplied to local undertakers. As time went on, the coffin making became more sophisticated and were distributed nationwide. Most undertakers were publicans and added their own finishings e.g., gold handles etc. Extra machinery was introduced as the business progressed and as the business grew, coffin panels were exported to the UK, Northern Ireland, Scotland, Belgium and Holland. As part of moving the business along, Matt travelled to China, New Zealand, India, Taiwan, Sweden and most European Countries sourcing raw materials and new equipment.

Hurling

Matt started playing hurling in Killyon, Co. Meath. He played in the Minor Hurling Championship and when he was 16 played senior hurling with Raharney. For a few years they didn't have a team, so he joined Cullion for two years. He was invited to a meeting in Raharney School and was offered Captaincy of Raharney and also Chairperson of Raharney Hurling Club, if he returned to play with them. Also, at that meeting, it was agreed that the club would purchase a Nissan Hut from a company in Monaghan. Matt travelled to purchase the hut, and it was installed in the field where the existing National School is now. Bill Geoghegan built the frame and Matt and a few of the committee members put in the seating, wiring, floor and stage. The hut was a good source of entertainment in the village. On one occasion Matt recalls he organized with Castlepollard Drama Society to put on a play – 'Able Dealer' and on many an evening the crowd would gather to watch a picture (movie).

Matt was chairperson of the club from 1955 until they won the senior hurling Championship in 1964. Matt loved his time on the playing field and can tell many a story. When reading through the newspaper archives his daughter found the following report written in the Westmeath Examiner after Raharney lost to Pearse's in the County Final of 1962. Footnote:- All praise to Raharney's Matt Gartland who, great sportsman that he is, found time to come along to the presentation of the Cup to Matty Mullen to add his congratulations and remain for Commandt. O'Callaghan's address. Certainly, an act of sportsmanship that Raharney may well be proud of. For "When the one great writer comes, to write against your name; He'll ask not that you won or lost, but how you play the game". Matt remembers these words often with pride and gives the same advice now to his grandchildren.

Matt would like to acknowledge the late Simon Coyne who picked up players and supporters in his truck to bring them to the hurling matches.

Building Contracts

In c.1961 the first milk powder plant in the Country was built in Killashandra, Co. Cavan. Jimmy Rooney was part of that. Paul Maxwell was the timekeeper. There were twenty-two people working two shifts on the project/scheme. Matt was the foreman.

Matt built the tan yard in Kinnegad, for the Dunne family c.1960, the Bank of Ireland in Killucan & Enfield and the Hardware Merchants in Kilcock 1964.

Matt married Linda Dunne in June 1970. A nurse from Shane, Edenderry, Co Offaly. When they got married Linda had to give up her job as in those days that was the law. She moved to Raharney and they had two children John & Elaine.

Today

Matt still goes to work every day at 7am after saying his prayers. He finishes at 4:30 pm. to drive home as he now lives with Elaine, before the busy traffic from Shay Murtagh's. take to the roads. He still employs six people making panelling for export to the UK and the Irish market.
Matt Gartland is a legend of his time, venturing into unchartered territory, withstanding all hardships leaving behind a legacy of skills and accomplishments. We are proud to say he is a true Raharney gentleman.

© *Rita Monaghan*

Looking Back Over The Centuries

Looking back now over the centuries, and the many hardships that have been endured by the Irish People. During almost 4 centuries since the first map and survey of Ireland and the awful deeds of Cromwell. There has been much hardship imposed on the Irish people through high land rents, evictions, the Penal Times, the Tithe land tax, and the Potato Famine Ireland suffered greatly at the hands of the British Government and landlords who had the support of the law of the land behind them. The people of Raharney and surrounding districts no doubt would have shared in this suffering. The Tithe Land tax which was introduced nationally between 1823 and 1837 was a tax on all land to support the protestant church. The records for all townlands in the Killucan Parish show what each land holder was obliged to pay. The rate was 9d per acre for 1st quality land and 6d an acre for 2nd. This might not seem much now but back then it was exceptionally difficult to pay. Many people resented it and did not pay it.

Below is a list of the people who were liable to pay The Tithe tax, this is taken from the Applotment list and all names are written as the appear on that list:

Ballinahee: *All were small holdings the average size was 5 acres and were all tenants of Lord Longford. In the year 1830 had 35 land holders listed -* James Keff, Patrick Keff, Laurence Delamer, William lovely, James Corcoran, Michael Larigan, Mathew Dangan, James Dangan, Betty Robinson, Anne Bray, Thomas Oxley, John Oxley James Coyne, Laurence Coyne, Patt Bruton, James Karney, Chris Coyne,James Murphy, Chris Lynch, James Lynch, Patt Bray, James Bray, Darby Ivory, Andrew Lynch ,Bryan Kairman, WidowB Burns, Patt Hughes, William Casserly, William Bray, Patt Neil, Edward Robinson, John Carney Richard Malone, Mathew Gavask.

Grangebeg:

Grangemore Estate:
780 acres

Thomas Maguire	9 acres	Lockard Ramage	90 acres,
Widow Maguire	2 acres	John Robinson	25 acres
James Goonery	16 acres	Robert Eginton	25 acres The Widow
Arthur Swords	9 acres	Eginton	37 acres
Frank Cavanagh	4 acres	Jonathan Tilson	77 acres
Edward Darigan	7 acres	Thomas Gibson	44 acres
Micheal Darigan	9 acres	Protestant Schoolhouse	1 acre
Edward Lynch	8 acres		
William Moran	4 acres		
Thomas Kenny	2 acres		
Patrick Darigan	8 acres		
Andrew Holdright	25 acres		

The Potato Famine and straightening the bends on the River Deel

The biggest disaster in Irish history was the potato Famine from 1845 to 1849.The failure of the potato crop, which was the stable diet of the poor, which made up a large majority of the Irish people. It was a shocking time in Ireland. There is no doubt the policies of the British government and the behavior of some landlords was responsible for many deaths, starvation, and misery suffered by the Irish people. Because they allowed a large amount of food to be exported from a country deep in a famine situation, this speaks for itself.

Three million live cattle, and large amounts of grain were exported to England during the famine years. While there was lots of alternative food available instead of potatoes. The barns of landlords and large farmers had lots of grain. Fields full of livestock, cattle, cows, sheep, and pigs. The rivers and lakes full of fish, some would ask 'Why was there a famine?'. There is no doubt this alternative food was denied to the starving people. A soup kitchen was set up for brief time and it did help a bit but should have continued for a much longer period
 The people of Raharney experienced some of this hunger misery and hardship. Some local families sold whatever property they had and immigrated to England and America.
Much has been written about this terrible time in Ireland when 1.5 million people died nationally and another million emigrated from Ireland. In 1851, as the Great Famine was ending, the population of Ireland had dropped to 6.5 million people. The Famine and the resulting Irish diaspora had a huge effect on the Irish population; by 1891, Ireland's population had slipped under five million and by 1931, it had dropped to just over four million. By the 1950's the population was at its lowest on record at two point nine million. The population of Raharney before the famine was approximately 3 times what it is now.

Rather than give any relief directly to the starving Irish people the British Government changed its policies and decided to make the starving people work for any relief they would provide. Needless famine relief schemes were dreamed up that were of no benefit to anyone whatsoever. Building roads that literally led nowhere but death for some who died on the job from hunger and disease.

Straightening the bends on the river Deel 400 meters upstream from the village of Raharney is a prime example of a totally needless scheme. This would have been a major task even with the machinery that's available today. This involved digging a new river channel about 300 meters long 12 meters wide and 4 meters deep. Removing approx. 10,000 tons of soil. The local people who worked on this scheme with only pick and shovel and wheelbarrows, worked in all-weather, freezing cold, half-dressed and probably in bare feet and sick with disease all while starving with hunger. Four pence a day was what the men were paid to buy food for their families.

There is anecdotal evidence of men only having a slice of raw turnip with a dust of meal to eat. This was the type of food that was generally fed to animals. There are stories told of men coming long distances looking for work sometimes to no avail. Standing beside the job waiting for someone to die to get their place. This was a cruel living hell for local people.

This unbelievable scheme resulted only in causing many deaths and great misery to many. It also affected a local landowner access to all his land. This resulted in the construction of a substantial wooden bridge, to allow him access. This bridge in later years was known as Whites wooden bridge when Whites became owners of this piece of land. The bridge remained there for 130 years until 1975-6 when it was removed by the O.P.W. when sinking the river.
 A similar but larger scheme was carried out further upstream where a bridge was also built over the river and was known as Hugh Lambs bridge it was also removed in 1975-6. A famine burial site is said to be somewhere in this location, which is not surprising. Repairs to the stone bridge and walls in the village of Raharney was also carried out in 1975-6. On a much lighter note, the older generation will remember Whites Bridge, as a great place for swimming and diving in the 50s and 60s where Nicky White, and Pat Murray the (Black Tread) used to give diving exhibitions.

© Shay Callaghan

(Left) This original Famine Pot was used in the village to distribute soup to the starving people.

(Above) This map of the River Deel shows the bend that was straightened during the Famine.

The Murrays

The Murrays are an old family of Raharney, all tracing back to at least one common ancestor bearing that surname in the 18th century. The Murrays owned farmland, but they relocated to cottages on Pudden Row around the time of the famine. Two of the Murrays married members of the White family. Timothy Murray was a cobbler/bootmaker.

Patrick Murray (Raharney - born late 1790s) married Christian Bray (Raharney - born late 1790s) their son Timothy Murray (Raharney – baptised 6th January 1831) married Margaret White (Raharney) on July 24, 1863. On the 5th March 1871 their son Christopher was baptised in Raharney and as an adult emigrated to New York where he married Mary Casserly (Croboy, Hill of Down, Co. Meath) in New York on September 5, 1898, and following her death in 1918 he married Mary Donohue. Christopher and Mary Casserly had seven children.

Christopher J. Murray (Jr.) (Born 1899)   **James T. Murray** (Born 1901)
Harry A. Murray (Born 1903)   **John F. Murray** (Born 1905)
Margaret M. Murray (Born 1907)   **Matthew P. Murray** (Born 1912)
Agnes E. Murray (Born 1915)

Christopher Murray:

Christopher had 9 siblings Christina, Patrick, Thomas, John, Joseph, Matthew, Michael, Mary, and James. Most of Christopher's siblings emigrated to New York. Of those that stayed in Ireland, Patrick Murray who was a cobbler was the only one to remain in the Pudden Row house in Raharney. He lived in it by himself unmarried until he suffered a crippling accident that eventually led to his death in 1930.

When Christopher Murray was 16, he moved to Dublin as apprentice for James D'Arcy. D'Arcy, who hailed from the wealthy D'Arcy family of Raharney, had opened a pub and grocery store at 20 Commons Street, in Dublin. For a brief time, he worked for the real-life Larry O'Rourke (as made famous in Ulysses) in Dublin, as a bartender. In 1894 he emigrated to New York where among his many achievements:

- He was a freelance American correspondent for the Westmeath Examiner for nearly 40 years using the pen name "Raharney Rover" in his younger years.
- He was an executive of the Westmeath Men's Social & Benevolent Association of New York City for nearly 40 years
- He was a co-founder of the United Irish Counties Association of New York, which is still around to this day. He was a referee, coach, and organiser of Gaelic Football and Track in New York.
- He invited the first ever film crew to Raharney. In 1929, famous Irish film producer Emmet Moore shot a film in Raharney at Christopher's urging.
- He co-organised a massive American return to Westmeath in 1932 for the Eucharistic Congress.
- He was a referee, coach, and organizer of Gaelic Football and Track in New York.

His brother Michael played for the Riverstown Emmets who won the Gaelic Football Championship in 1907. (He died of Tuberculosis in 1908).

One of his sons, James Murray, was the most famous movie star in the world for a time. His breakout film, The Crowd, was released in 1928. James was in more than two dozen films, some silent, but mostly talkies. It was argued that James Murray was the only man with Westmeath blood that was more famous at the time, than John McCormack.

Patsy Murray's, Raharney.

Christopher Murray who was hugely involved in the Irish Community in New York, retained his love for his native Raharney. His support for the community in Raharney is nowhere more evident than in St. Bridget's Church, where the commemorative Holy Water Font is located. He was a co-founder of the Raharney Rovers of New York City and helped raise funds for Raharney Church, which was heavily damaged by a large storm in 1903. Raharney Rovers of New York City organised fundraising events for the restoration. These events were well supported by exiles from Raharney and the surrounding areas of Rathwire, Killucan, Coralstown, Kinnegad and Mullingar.

The proceeds from these events were used to purchase the beautiful stained-glass windows behind the altar still bearing the inscription "Erected to the of God by the Raharney Rovers, New York"

James and Harry Murray:

James was extremely interested in acting, having worked as a door attendant on Broadway. After some small parts, he decided to travel to Los Angeles. His younger brother Harry went with him traveling sometimes on freight trains and hitch-hiking. Harry got tired of this and decided to go back to New York although he eventually ended up in Los Angeles in the film industry.

James arrived in California eventually. He had several different jobs before he managed to get work as a film extra. He was noticed by a director named Vidor who liked his looks and wanted someone to portray an everyday man in a new film. James Murray's portrayal of Johnny Sims in a film called "The Crowd" was outstanding in the era of silent films. James also had parts in the film "Rose Marie." He appeared alongside such famous actors as John Wayne, James Stewart, and Shirley Temple. Unfortunately, James suffered from depression and alcoholism. He was trick acting one day beside the Hudson River in New York and fell in, and by the time he was recovered he was dead. He died in 1936.

Harry Murray, James's brother having decided to return to New York was not finished with acting, however, Harry arrived in Los Angles. He worked as an extra and then got a part in a film 'The House of Scandal' in 1928. He was like his brother James in appearance, and this proved a disadvantage in the silent film era. He went back to Broadway where he starred in musicals by Irving Berlin and Jerome Kern and had his own dance troupe 'The Debonairs.' Harry achieved his greatest success on early TV C.B.S. He produced the long running games show 'To Tell the Truth'. He retired from C.B.S. in 1968. In his retirement he volunteered for 28 years working at a hospital in Carmel, New York where he was known and loved by all. Harry Murray died in 2002 in New York. R.I.P.

© Rita Monaghan

(Left) Christopher Murray with his 2nd wife (Muddie), daughter Agnes Murray and son James Murray aboard the SS Seagate off the coast of New York while James prepares to go on set to act out his role in The Crowd (1928).

The Raharney Rovers

The Raharney Rovers Social Club Founded in New York in 1895 by a group of Westmeath emigrants mainly from Raharney and was absorbed into the Westmeath Men's Social & Benevolent Association of New York in 1911. The Club may well have taken the name from the Raharney Rovers football team which existed in 1890's prior to their emigration. Raharney Rovers later returned as a hurling club in 1904.

Original Organisation: -
President: Christopher J. Flanagan, born October 14, 1871, Raharney
Secretary: Christopher J. Murray, baptized March 5, 1871, Raharney
Affiliated Men: Patrick Flanagan, John Flanagan, John Murray, Joseph Grattan, James Grattan, John Fitzsimons, Michael Fitzsimons, F. McKenna, Charles McKenna, Charles Hughes, Thomas Hughes, Walter Tobin, John O'Brien, John Shaughnessy, Patrick Garty, William Kilduff, Joseph Creighton, Mr. Swords, Eddie Made, M. Shelly, J. Shelly, P. Smyth.
Affiliated Ladies: Anne Whyte, Mary Whyte, Annie Russell, Jennie Coyne, Annie Montgomery, Maggie Murphy, Julia Lynch, Kate Barns, Katie Hoey, Mary Flanagan, Jennie Keane, Ms. Manning, Mrs. Kilduff, Ms. McNamee.
Clubhouse: 37 East 42nd Street, New York, New York.
Club Song & Dance: "Pudden Row"
Club Parishes: St. Gabriel Church, 310 East 37th Street, New York, New York
St. Agnes Church, 143 East 43rd Street, New York, New York

Sources: Westmeath Examiner (Ireland). The Advocate (New York)

The church in Raharney was heavily damaged by a large storm in 1903. Along with hosting concerts to raise funds for a restoration, the parish also invited The Most Rev. Dr. Higgins, Bishop of Rockhampton, in Australia (who was a former priest in Westmeath) to travel all the way to Rathwire to drum up even more financial support. Though a substantial amount of funds were raised, local residents were still dealing with their own financial woes caused by the very same storm. Given the circumstances, St. Mary's schoolmaster John Kelly and Raharney District Councillor Nicholas White collaborated with Raharney's Rev. Dr. Dooley on sending an appeal to the Raharney Rovers of New York City for assistance. This account and the events that followed were well documented. Today, the stained-glass windows that stand by the altar still bear the inscription *"Erected to the glory of God by the Raharney Rovers, New York."*

Westmeath Examiner: July 22, 1905
Written by: Christopher J. Murray, aka Christie Murray, aka Raharney Rover
Published August 26, 1905

Dear Sir,

Permit me to thank you, through the columns of your paper, on behalf of the Raharney Rovers of New York, for the excellent reproduction of the design of the windows of Raharney Chapel in your issue of July 22nd, thereby bringing them before the exiled sons and daughters of Raharney, and showing to what an extent the funds that were collected by them, were used. They also desire to return thanks to Very Rev. Dr. Dooley for his kind consideration of them in allowing the funds to be used in a manner that will remain as an everlasting monument to the zeal, loyalty, and generosity of those who contributed towards their erection.

I wish, also to call your attention to the note at foot of illustration, which states, "That my brother and I have forwarded cheques in two instalments" This is, I am sure, an unintentional error. The fact is every Rover in New York and a good many outside of it, who came a long distance to testify by their presence and their mite to the noble work, and to show their appreciation of and devotion to the worthy efforts of those at home, and the credit lies in the efforts of no individual one, but in the unity of all. The cause was a just one. It was the first appeal of its kind that was ever made on behalf of Raharney Chapel.

When the appeal was made through Mr. John Kelly, N T, and Sir Nicholas White, Rev Dr. Dooley was practically a stranger to most of the Rovers, but through the work that he had already accomplished in arranging settlements between landlords and tenants in connection with the Land Purchase Bill and other transactions of a similar nature in the parish, he had become well known and popularly spoken of. On that account, and on account of the ties that bind the Rovers so closely to their dear native village by the Deel, it was easy to set the wheels in motion. While the Rovers so gallantly did their part, they were ably assisted by almost all the young, exiled men, and Women of Rathwire and Killucan. Mullingar was not back ward in supporting the good work, no more than were Coralstown and Kinnegad.

We were indebted to Rev Dr. Brann (who is a native of Ballivor) for the use of his School Hall in which to hold our first entertainment and to Mr Michael J Jennings (who is a Mullingar man) for the privilege of holding our second entertainment and dance.

The thanks of every Rover at home and in exile is due to the Editor of the "Irish American Advocate" for leaving its columns at our disposal and publishing notices of our entertainment several weeks before it came off, which aided us materially in bringing it before the public. So, you see Raharney, even in exile, can count on a host of friends. Best of all, the arrangements in both cases were so complete there was not a hitch to mar the pleasure of those that attended, and apart from the worthy object of the affair, it was a beautiful sight to see the assemblage sons and daughters of Westmeath together, where they met the playmates of their childhood, the companions of their youth, and their friends of later years. There in the fulness of their hearts they enjoyed themselves in a manner that could not be duplicated. Among them the proverbial Irish greeting was extended, and the hearty Irish laugh that at one time rang through the rafters of the old homestead were heard, and the sweet strains of native Irish music on the bagpipes, the violin, and the harp, all blending together, the melodies of our own country, unequalled, unsurpassed in any place in the wide, wide world, and to be found only in that one spot –

"Which is first flower of the earth, And first gem of the sea."

It is needless for me for to assure you, Mr Editor that the nights were wholly Irish nights, that the music, the dancing, the songs and recitations were the products of Irish masters. As it is the strongest desire of the Westmeathian in exile to keep up with the pace that is set by their brothers at home, an example of which is found in the issue of the EXAMINER of July 8 in connection with the "Kinnegad Aeridheacht," which certainly deserves the commendation of every Irishman at home and abroad.

In conclusion, I will again ask you to make the necessary correction, and by doing so you will confer an everlasting obligation on

Yours truly,
Christie Murray (Raharney Rover)

In 1892, Christopher won two notable competitions, one was to submit a drawing of an Irish Cottage and another of a Mill Wheel. The Weekly Freeman published both in its newspaper that year. ©

Nancy Flynn

(Left) Bishop Michael Smith, Nancy Flynn and Rev. Monsignor Eamon Marron on the occasion of the presentation of the Benemerenti Medal to Nancy in Raharney Church in 1994. *(Right)* The Benemerenti Medal is awarded by the Pope to members of the clergy and laity in recognition for service to the Catholic Church. Nancy spent 49 years as sacristan looking after Raharney Church and the clergy.

The Deel & Boyne Anglers' Association

The Deel & Boyne Anglers' Association is an organization that has survived to preserve the River Deel and improve/control fishing.

The Association was founded under the title–The Deel Trout Anglers' Association on Friday, 23rd August, 1935. A Committee was formed which included both male and female members.

It was in the following year, 1936, that the name was changed to the Deel & Boyne Anglers' Association. On that night, a committee member proposed that a stretch of the River Boyne rented by him should be controlled by the Association and this was agreed upon by all members.

The Association thrived and membership grew steadily from 1935 to the late 1960's. It was then that membership began to decline due to the Boyne Drainage Scheme which decimated the waters. The Scheme caused mediocre fishing and membership dived to an all-time low. The continuance of the Club at that time relied upon the perseverance of a few resolute members. They kept the Club in existance by paying the Water Rates during those lean years. Fortunately, membership began to increase in the late 1970's and continued to do so until 2011. Membership then again began to decline and has continued to do so, current membership is approximately forty.

Restocking of the water occurred in 2007-2009, when the Club invested in three hundred large fish and 20,000 Summerlings. An Enhancement Project took place on the river in October 2021, to improve spawning beds for Salmon, Trout and Lamprey, and the habitat of all creatures living there. Pool and gravel areas have been installed to restore habitats and provide important ecological niches for Trout and Salmon in various stages of their lifecycles. Stockproof fencing will promote the growth of Riverine plants which help the water quality, as they serve as a buffer zone, to suck up the excessive run of nutrients. This will make the river more robust in its fight against Climate Change.

The Enhancement Project will also benefit the wider Ecological Community, including Otters, Kingfishers, Lamprey, Crayfish, insect life and a host of other species that rely upon the insects.

The Annual Pike Fishing Competition for the Jack Shaw (former secretary) Memorial Trophy is open to both junior and senior members. There is also an Annual Trout Fishing Competition which is open to all members.

The current Chairman is Michael Tedders and Club Secretary is Paddy Connaughton.

© Paddy Connaughton

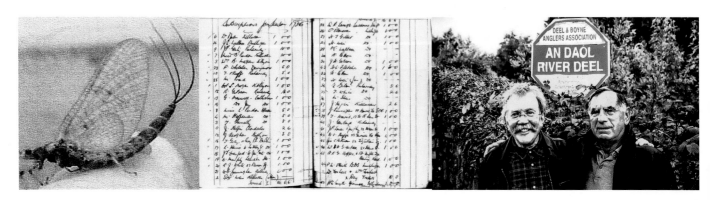

Westmeath United Coursing Club

Since the foundation of the Club in 1925, Westmeath United Coursing has become one of the most popular meetings of the early coursing season.

Although we started in Killucan ninety-six years ago, coursing now takes place in Raharney. In the early 1950's Westmeath United moved from Higginstown to Curristown where we coursed on land owned by Billy Dunne on the Killucan-Raharney Road, where we remained for twenty-seven years. In the early 1980's we moved to Riverdale, Raharney and coursing was held on land by our own then Secretary of the Club, Brendan Farrelly. There we have remained and will this year celebrate our ninety-sixth year of our famous Belsize Cup Meeting.

Westmeath United lives on and the members look forward to their three-day festival each October. Coursing today faces many challenges; however, it has a good number of dedicated supporters, and it is these together with a strong promotional campaign that can secure its future. We are greatly indebted to our founder members who inaugurated this Club ninety-six years ago. Each year we run four stakes - 'The Belsize All Age Cup', 'The Ber Murtagh Memorial Derby', 'The Paddy Farrelly Memorial Oaks', and for our working members 'The Paddy Mulvaney Memorial Stake'

© Dolores Carr

Juvenile Nominators 1990: Pictured with Eileen Farrelly and Tommy Eggerton are Paula McCormack, Serena O'Connor, Tresa Shaw, Aoife Farrelly, Elizabeth Shaw, Gemma Shiels, Darren Murtagh, Ger Byrne, Daniel Murtahg, Lorraine Carr, Pauric McCormack, Emma Leech, Ronan O'Connor, Orlaith Farrelly, Finian Farrelly, Declan Carr, Oliver Byrne, and Ronan McCormack.

G. Hassel, B. Keenan, J. Casserly, J. Cullen, M. Horan, T. Taylor, T. Harte, P. Smyth, P. Keegan, J. Clyne, T. Cox, D. Fitzpatrick, Fr. Mahon, Carlow, Master Harte, P. Flynn, J. Meehan, J. Bruton and P. Kearney,

WESTMEATH UNITED CC FOUNDER MEMBERS

Back row: Slipper: P. Reynolds, P. Timmons, A. Daly, J. Mc. Cormack, B. Mc. Hugh, B. O' Shaughnessy, T. Mc.Namee, P. Flynn, W. Rooney, T. Eggerton, T. Murtagh, D. Carr, J. Tuize, M. Leech, P. Gaffney, J. Tuize, P. Mulvanney, G. Ivory, G. Leech, D. Carrr, B. Murtagh, A. Leech, K. Carr.

Front Row: D. Carr, R. Mc.Cormack, C. Mc. Cormack, K. Ivory, R. Walsh, H. Leech, N. Leech, N. Farrelly, J. Glynn, B. Leech

Vincent Smyth, MRCVS

Vincent, a native of Ringtown, Castlepollard, qualified from UCD as a vet in 1960. In 1965, he moved to Raharney with his wife Deirdre and set up a mixed practice from their home. Vincent is well known and respected in Raharney and the surrounding community, having helped and advised many farmers young and old and at all times of the day and night!

In addition to treating and caring for animals in his professional capacity as a vet, Vincent thoroughly enjoyed and valued the many friendships he made with clients over the years. One of the more unusual happenings in the bovine world was the birth of quadruplet calves, born to a cow belonging to Willie Doyle, Craddenstown.

In February, 2011, Vincent received a silver medal from the Verinary Council of Ireland honouring more than 5 years service to the vetinary profession. He continue to practice until his retirement in December 2020, marking more than 60 years of service.

© Deirdre Smyth

One in a Million!

WESTMEATH EXAMINER, SATURDAY, JULY 10, 1976

What may constitute an Irish record was established on the farm of Mr. Willie Doyle, Craddenstown, Raharney, when a Cross Hereford cow gave birth to four calves, pictured above with Mrs. Doyle and daughter Marie. Mr. Doyle purchased three cross-bred heifer calves at Trim Mart in 1973 at £25 each. The mother, above, was one of these and she had her first calf in the Autumn of 1975. She was inseminated on October 11th last to the performance proven Hereford bull, Ardmulchan Jumbo, from Athboy AI Station. On June 30th last she gave birth to three bull and one heifer calf—all are doing well.

We inquired from County Westmeath Committee of Agriculture as to the rarity of quadruplet calves. Records available show that approx. two per cent of calves are twins. There are no records of quad calves born in the county, but it was felt that the chances are one in a couple of millions. Dr. Patrick Cunningham, who specialises in animal genetics at the Agricultural Institute is checking the records on the occurrence of quad calves.

Scouting

Lir District

Scout Association of Ireland (S.A.I) Lir District covered County Westmeath around the Mullingar area. The four swans are the Children of Lir from the old Celtic legend. The badge was issued in two varieties, one with a dark grey backing, the other had a white backing. There was no difference in the design on the front of the badge.

(Above)
Killucan-Raharney Scouts:
Judy O'Gorman
Peter Austin
Frances Fitzsimons
Mary Briody
Anne Maher
Maureen O'Neill.
(Left)
Lir District badge.

Weddings

(Top left)
Nicky Weir &
Olive Geoghegan
(Raharney) 23rd May 1966.

(Top middle)
Nellie & Liam Geoghegan
26th September 1942.

(Top right)
Paddy Connaughton &
Lillie Sheils
1966.

(Middle left)
Noel Weir &
Una Cusack.

(Middle right)
Eamonn & Rosaleen (nee Cusack) Hickey
(Raharney) 31st March 1963.

(Bottom left)
Frank & Annie
McHugh.

(Bottom right)
Mickey Flanagan & Ina Flynn.

"House For Sale"

Perched upon a ladder
Suppressing a pensive smile
An attic packed with memories
Items scattered, mayhem style.

Vintage vacuum cleaners
School books on a bulky shelf
Handwritten cut-throat recipes
Exquisite china, inconsequential delph.

Trapped in a corner
Against a cobwebbed wall
John F. Kennedy kept vigil in our kitchen
Eamon de Valera surveilled our hall.

The Sacred Heart with glowing lamp
Vinyl records in a stack
Cuddly dolls and teddy bears
Now labelled 'bric-a-brac'

Lingering on this step ladder
Fond memories reappear
God help me to surrender
To the passing of the years.

Anne Maher ©

|Image: Arc Studios|

GAA

Camogie

Our records indicate that camogie was dominant in Raharney as far back as 1933-34. After a spell of non-activity it took a resurgence in the early 1960s, resulting in an impressive Junior Championship win in 1966.

Westmeath Camogie board disbanded county camogie in 1968 and it wasn't until 1978 that it was revived, Raharney fielded U14 and Junior teams at this time. The club grew exponentially over the next 3 decades, with various levels of success:-

U14 Feile	U14
From 1980 to 2022	From 1980 to 2022
Represented Westmeath on a host of occasions with our greatest achievement in **2013** **ALL IRELAND WINNERS**	A plethora of wins, the most recent in October 2022 with a very impressive win over Lough Lene Gaels
Minor Great success over the year	

Senior Camogie

From 1978 to 1985 Senior Camogie grew from strength to strength, culminating in a massive county title in 1985, it would be another 22 years before the girls in blue lifted a trophy again. This win in 2015 would prove to be the catalyst for a host of glory days with a straight run of wins from 2015 to 2022.

Just a few highlights from our many successes......

2018 – In a pulsating win over an emerging Clonkill team, the final played in Kinnegad on the 22 Sept 2018 result in Raharney 3-9 Clonkill 2-7. Elaine Finn and Aoife Doherty were the goalscorers with a youthful Amelia Shaw picking up player of the match. Andreanna Doyle (Tiny) was presented with the cup by John Weir (Board Chairman).

2020 – Raharney outclassed their opponents and emerged victorious on a scoreline of Raharney 8-14 to Clonkill 0-02. Aoife Doherty picked up player of the match and was also joint captain with her sister Laura. In the All Ireland Semi Final and a very close contest against Glen Watty Grahams our girls in blue came away with a win Raharney 0-09 to Glen 1-04 and marched on to the All Ireland Final.

The All Ireland Final took place on Sunday the 9th January 2021 in Moyne Templetuohy GAA in County Tipperary. These warriors from Raharney led by Padraic Connaughton got off to the best possible start when Hannah Core goaled in the first few minutes. The exchanges were extremely physical and despite Clanmaurice surging ahead in the 3rd quarter, the girls dug deep and came away with THE WIN. Raharney 1-7 Clanmauric 0-7. Hannah Core picked up player of the match.

Padraic Connaughton, his management team and his Senior Camogie Warriors are ALL IRELAND CHAMPIONS and are written into the history books of Camogie!

Whilst we have had an abundance of exceptional players over the years, we pay a special tribute to our greatest ever camogie player Pamela Greville, Throughout her star-studded career Pamela won numerous club titles, represented Leinster in the Interprovincial series, and won many individual awards including 2 Soaring Stars and the 2019 WGPA Intermediate Player of the Year accolade.

Many of our past players are sadly no longer with us, and we remember and acknowledge all of their contributions. One lady in particular Kathy Duffy but fondly known to most of us as Kathy McKeogh played in the 1930s but also on the 1966 Junior winning team. Kathy attended many camogie games over the years and had great anecdotes and sayings (not all of them suitable for printing 💩), her most favourite was "A sure a hen could hit it further than that"

RAHARNEY
WESTMEATH CAMOGIE CHAMPIONS, 1966

Back row, l. to r., Lil Quinn, Marie Greville, Tess McKeon, Rose Dargan, Kathy Heffernan, Mary Price.
Front row, l. to r., Mary Doyle, Lucy Quinn, Anne Lynam, Frances Price, Lily Connaughton, Anne Doyle.

Back Row: Kathy McKeogh, Lillie Sheils, Annette Colman, Lil Quinn, Lily Keena, Rosaleen Dargan, Kathy Geoghegan, Frances Price, Ann Rooney
Front: Josie McKeogh, Kathy Heffernan, Theresa Molligan, Ollie Geoghegan, Imelda Lynam

Under 12's Champions (early 80's)

All Ireland Champions 2020
(Back L-R) Fiona Leavy, Katryn Nea, Niall Flanagan, Teresa Lynch, Sarah Kiernan, Anna Weir, Aoife Boyle, Aisling Doyle, Jade McKeogh, Maria Kelly, Katie Coleman, Cathy Doyle, Megan Weir-Hall, Liz Raleigh, Saoirse McGee, Megan Carroll, Aisling Keogh, Caoimhe McAteer, Sarah Coleman, Padraic Connaughton.
(Front L-R) Erin Core, Amelia Shaw, Muireann Brady (mascot) Amee Nea, Meadhbh Monaghan, Ellen Shaw, Ciara Keogh, Niamh Brady, Aoife O'Malley, Laura Doherty, Aoife Doherty, Elaine Finn, Andreanna Doyle, Mary Geraghty, Hannah Core.

All Ireland Champions 2013
Back L-R) Liz Shaw, Rachel Glennon, Emma Patton, Jodie Melhorn, Ruth O'Connor, Ellen Cronin, Nicola Cunneen, Erica Conway, Ciara O'Looney, Megan Carroll, Aine Brady, Kayleigh Monaghan, Gemma Swords, Jade McKeogh, Aileen Lawlor, (President Camogie Association).
(Front L-R) Niamh Doyle, Mary Dunne, Aoife O'Malley, Aoife Doherty, Hannah Core, Aoife Doherty, Sarah Guinan, Orla Quinn, Amelia Shaw, Katie Coleman, Meadhbh Smith, Jo Giles.

Hurling

Like many areas in Ireland in the 1800's cricket was played in the parish, teams usually represented the local landlord of the area and played neighboring landlords for wagers.

Raharney Hurling Club as it is known today was established initially as a football club (for branch as clubs were originally known) and was known as Raharney Rovers Football Club. Some members who emigrated to New York in the early 1900's sent back money to put in the lovely stained-glass windows behind the altar in Saint Bridgit's Church, Raharney. Riverstown Emmets were formed in the early 1900's and had their home games played in Sharry's field on the Mullingar Road before moving to Riverstown, near Cunningham's public house in 1907. The rise of Rivertown Emmets contributed to the demise of Raharney Rovers as a football team however they reinvented themselves as a hurling team in 1904 with the help of two men from Tipperary who were working on the renovation of Saint Bridget's Church, Raharney. Tom and Joe Maher along with local man Peter Nea were instrumental in laying the foundation stone for a Raharney hurling club as we know it today.

In the early 1900's Harris's field, a short distance outside the village on the Ballivor road was the home ground for the Club. Raharney participated in the junior championship in those early years and in 1912 achieved victory in the junior final, our first major honor. The following year, 1913 Raharney Rovers were victorious in the senior championship final, the first final of the club. They defeated Crookedwood on a score line of 3-4 to 1-0. In 1914 the club won the second title by defeating Castlepollard Sarsfieldson on a score line of 5-1 to 0-0.

A break of a few years saw us waiting until one year after WW1 to win our 3rd title defeating Drumraney. Remarkably that was to be Raharney Rovers last win in the senior championship for a staggering 48 years. The 20's, 30's and 40's were lean years for the Club, and it was not until 1947 that a number of men revitalized the club's fortunes, men like Hughie Flanagan, Tommy Farrelly (local shoemaker whose skills were often used to mend the leather hurling balls) Pat Price and local postman, Bill Raleigh. In the early 1950's the Club played and trained for a short time in Reilly's field (beside Ashcroft Park) before moving to Joristown Park in 1955.

Deelsiders' joy as Under 14s reclaim Feile title

Canon Fogarty Trophy returns to Raharney

Coilin Duffy

RAHARNEY Under 14 hurlers completed the midlands set of back-to-back All-Ireland Feile na nGael Division 2 doubles, following in the footsteps of Portlaoise and Birr on Sunday at Pearse Stadium, Galway.

Joint captains and twins, Ciaran and Killian Doyle starred in the final as Raharney overcame Portlaoise in the decider by 4-9 to 1-3.

Remarkably this scoreline was just one-point shy of the 4-10 to 1-3 result against Down side, Bredagh in last year's final at Cusack Park, Ennis.

As was the case 12 months ago Killian Doyle had a big say on the scoring front in Raharney's quest to retain the Canon Fogarty Trophy.

Killian scored 4-6 out of the 4-9 tally in the final. In fact he claimed a massive 24 goals and 14 points over the weekend - a tally of 86 points, beating his record from last year.

Over the weekend, 3-26 of Raharney's scores were claimed by other players - Killian is truely a star of the future. A boy though with plenty of maturity on his young shoulders, and he was keen to point to the overall squad performance when speaking after the game. "It is all about the win, once we get over the line and win that's the main thing," he said. "It doesn't really matter about what I score, it is about the team.

"Only for the managers (we wouldn't be here). They put in so much commitment and everything we need you just ask and they get it for us.

"Declan Mullen and everyone are great for us. Declan is up at training every evening and only for him and all the managers we would have nothing."

Killian netted his opening goal after just 47 seconds of the decider, and by the 13th minute Raharney had led by 4-2 to 0-2.

Portlaoise pegged a goal back in injury time from Aaron Bergin to ensure a 4-4 to 1-2 interval scoreline.

Theo Broderick, Darragh Murray and Ciaran Doyle were the other scorers in the final for Raharney with Ciaran and Killian accepting the trophy from GAA President Christy Cooney after the game.

On the way to the final Raharney beat Meelick-Eyrecourt (10-6 to 3-3); Kiltormer (6-7 to 0-5) and Ballinscreen (3-11 to 0-4) in the group stages and Mount Leinster Rangers by 4-7 to 0-7 in the semi-final.

Raharney's quest for a Feile double was halted at the weekend, after the club's camogie team failed to reach the knockout stages of Division 3.

It was a brave bid by the squad, who rued a 0-2 to 0-0 defeat to Liam Mellows to deny them a top spot in Group C and a knockout stages berth.

On Friday afternoon Raharney claimed a 4-0 to 0-1 win over Castlegar, while on Saturday they were 2-5 to 2-1 victors over Kerry side, Causeway.

The Feile na nGael Hurling bandwagon rolls into Dublin next year, with the Feile Peil na nOg taking place this Thursday, Friday and Saturday in Cork.

Raharney Panel: Aaron McHugh, Conor Murray, Dylan Riggs, Conor Donoghue, Jack Duignan, Ciaran Doyle, Marc Gorman, Jamie Duignan, James Goonery, Jack Coyne, Theo Broderick, Darragh Murray, Dean Core, Killian Doyle, Donal Mullen, Graham Riggs, Neill Carthy, Eoin Keyes, Killian Farrelly, Darren Finn, Karl Farrelly, Shaun Moran, Brian McHugh, Robert Coyne.

Raharney Camogie Panel: April Rowley, Anna Weir, Kaithlyn Gardiner, Tess MacLachlon, Rachel Murphy, Rachel O'Malley, Megan Carroll, Maria Kelly, Aileen McHugh, Jade McKeogh, Laura Patton, Laura Doherty, Angel Rowney, Ashling Goss, Lara Mac Lochlon, Hannah Mae Granger, Emily Hart, Ciara Darby, Aine Brady, Nicola Cunneen, Niamh Smith, Aoife Dotherty, Emma Patton, Hannah Core.

SATURDAY, JULY 2, 2011 **29**

SPORT

Raharney captain, Killian Doyle raises aloft the Canon Fogarty trophy after the Westmeath champions successfully defended their National Feile na nGael crown in Pearse Park, Galway on Saturday.

The Raharney Under 14 team which retainted the Canon Fogarty trophy at the National Feile na nGael finals in Galway. Back row Paul Quinn, Jack Duignan, Ciaran Doyle, Darragh Murray, Theo Broderick, Aaron McHugh, Killian Doyle, Dylan Riggs, Graham Riggs, Jamie Duignan, Killian Farrelly, Eoin Keys, Jack Coyne, Michael Flanagan, Conor Murray and John Coyne. In front, from left, John Donoghue, Neil Carty, James Goonery, Dean Core, Karl Farrelly, Sean Moran, Darren Finn, Mark Gorman. Robert Coyne, Brian McHugh, Donal Mullen, Conor Donoghue, Michael Doyle.

Club Iomána Ratháirne

'THE BLUES'

VICTORY DINNER DANCE

FRIDAY 8th FEBRUARY, 1985

IN THE WORKMAN'S HALL

*A FINALE TO CENTENARY YEAR '84,
THE GREATEST YEAR IN THE HISTORY
OF THE CLUB*

RAHARNEY HURLING CLUB.

CEILI, OLD-TIME
PRESENTATION OF MEDALS
IN KILLUCAN HALL
ON FRIDAY, 1st MAY, 1964

MUSIC BY
JOE DELANEY AND HIS BAND

DANCING 9—2.

ADMISSION 5/-

WESTMEATH EXAMINER LTD., MULLINGAR

"THE BLUES"

*Get your Hurley and come to Raharney
To the top club in Westmeath.
From the playpen to the great men
We foster skill and guts and speed;
Senior, Junior and Under Twenty One
We showed all clubs how it should be done
Triple Champions — Club of the Year
The Mighty Blues are here*

TOASTS

MENU

Grapefruit and Mandarin Cocktail

***

Riverdale Farmhouse Soup

***

Roast Stuffed Turkey
&
Joristown Ham
(with Cranberry Sauce)

***

Craddenstown Carrots
Buttered Garden Peas
Creamed Deelside Potatoes

***

Centenary Trifle
with Triple Dream Topping

***

Tea or Coffee
and Victory Cake

***

Champagne

Raharney Seniors 1974.

Raharney Seniors 1976.

After many years in the junior ranks Raharney arrived on the senior scene once again and contested our first senior final for many years in 1962, lost by the narrowest of margins to Mullingar's Pearses on a score line of 2-09 to 3-05. However, Raharney gained revenge for that defeat with a win over Pearses in 1967. That historic winning team was Mickey Carr, Matt Mullen, Seamus Holdwright, Jack Shaw (Capt.), Joe Moore, Kevin Lynch, Jimmy Nugent, Pat Croach, Tony Donahue, Ray Smyth, Jimmy Rooney, Mickey Flanagan, Jimmy Weir, Nicky Weir and Brendan Sheils. Subs Sean Gaynor, Sean Greville, Kevin Carr, Ned McKeogh and Des McKeogh.

The next success at senior level was in 1973 when Raharney overcame Castlepollard to claim our 5th senior title. That team was Sean Greville, Frank Sheils, (Capt.) Seamus Holdwright, Jack Shaw, Donnie Smyth, Kevin Lynch, Jimmy Corroon, Peter Duignan, Pat Croach, Mickey Flanagan, Jimmy Nugent, Matt McKeogh, Jimmy Weir, Brian Murtagh and Nicky Weir. Subs Tony Donahue and Ray Smyth.
A lot of hard luck stories followed, losing 5 finals including 3 in a row 74,75,76,79 and 81. However in the background great work was being done at underage level by Seamus Brennan (in Raharney, National School) and Mickey Cannon, Tommy McKeogh and a host of willing helpers culminating in a lot of success at under 14 to minor level, with a win at senior level in 1984 (centenary year) Raharney overcame firm favorites Castletown Geoghegan in a thrilling final on a score line of 2-14 to 2-12 after which there was great scenes of joy after all the years of heartache. That successful team was Noel Greville, Declan Mullen, Thos Cleary, Declan Weir, Donnie Smyth, Martin Hickey, Michael Farrelly, Liam Lynch, Mattie Mullen, Joe Doyle, Michael Doyle, John Donoghue, Sean Greville, Frank Sheils, the captain on the day was the late John McManus RIP (whose death at such a young age was a huge loss to RHC).

An eight-year gap followed, winning again in 1992 captained by John Coyne (a final played in Castletown while Cusack Park was being renovated) defeating Lough Lene Gaels on a score line of 2-06 to 1-06. Once again captained by Anthony 'Gossy' Weir, Raharney won in 1994 (played in Collinstown) Ray Smyth as manager was a major driving force with these teams of this period along with Liam Lynch (physical trainer). A narrow defeat in 1995 to Castlepollard that was the last final for the club to contest until 2006.

Once again Raharney had to go back and rebuild from the bottom up by restructuring our underage teams, many men and women were involved in this process, but Declan Mullen was very much to the fore in everything and that was going on at this time. The 2006 win against Castletown Geoghegan, which went to a replay, captained by John Greville was reward for the underage development of the previous years. After the draw game on a score line of 1-09 each, Raharney made no mistake in the replay winning 4-05 to 2-05, our 9th title. Raharney were county champions again in 2008 captained by Niall Flanagan, defeating old rivals Clonkill 0-15 to 2-06. In 2010 captained by John Shaw we were champions once again defeating Clonkill in a very close and exciting finish on a score line of 2-14 to 1-16. It was during this period that Raharney enjoyed tremendous success at underage level, winning under 14 National Féile na nGael division 2 titles in 2010 (Clare) and 2011 (Galway).

Our senior team went on to win the senior title in 2014, captained by Conor Jordan, defeating Castlepollard 2-12 to 1-09 and 2016 when captained by Paul Greville.

With a score line of 2-18 to Clonkill 1-13 managed by Brendan McKeogh and captained by Sean Quinn we won again in 2021 against Castletown Geo. keeping up the great lucky tradition of Craddenstown winning captains.

The history of Raharney Hurling Club is not all about the winners of medals and cups. It's about the people who played during the lean years keeping the club alive, the supporters who cheered us on in good and bad times and contributed financially to the club, the committees who from the club's foundation built the great club we have today and most especially those who have given their time to foster and teach to our children the wonderful game that is hurling.

Scór

Raharney has a long and proud association with Scór in both Junior and Senior Levels. We have reached the Westmeath Finals in all events on many occassions and have gone on to represent the county several times.

Scór was established in 1969 with the aim of fostering Irish traditional pastimes while offering club members the chance to meet up, have fun and represent their club. The competition is divided into two age levels. Scór na nÓg for young people under seventeen years, and Scór Sinsir, for those over seventeen years. The competition brought focus and fun to Club members during the winter months when there was a pause in sporting events.

There are eight events in Scór that cover all aspects of Irish Culture.

- Céile Dancing
- Solo Singing
- Instrumental Music
- Recitation/Storytelling
- Ballad Group
- Novelty Act
- Set Dancing
- Question Time

Scór had a positive impact on the Community, encouraging sporting and non-sporting members in the area to showcase their talents. Whilst competitive in nature, what is remembered most is the fun, encouraging culture.

Throughout the years numerous members of the Community exhibited their talents on the stage. Helping them along the way in each category were

- Mary Cannon
- Eileen Keegan
- Tish Millar
- Nancy McKeogh
- Nell Geoghegan
- Margaret Farrelly
- Lillie Connaughton
- Olive Weir
- Tadgh Dineen
- Geraldine Flynn
- Noeleen Lynam
- Theresa Mooney
- Coll Doyle
- Shay Callaghan
- Tom Kiernan

We have so many happy memories of our history in the Scór Competitions.

Noeleen Lynam © Lisa Connaughton ©

(Left) Francis Farrell, Helen Connaughton, Martina McKeogh, Ger Flynn, Nicola Weir *(Middle Left)* Padraig Connaughton, Paul McKeogh, Niamh Callaghan, Gemma Weir, Jacinta Goonery, Nick Weir, David Cannon, Josephine Farrelly, Sarah Weir *(Right)* Una Weir Duggan.

Joristown GAA

TOPIC • 27 August, 2015

SIXTY YEARS IN THE MAKING
Joristown GAA park making great advances

Over the decades, since the Raharney Hurling Club first acquired Joristown GAA Park in the early 1950s, the club has spent a great deal of money in developing and improving the park situated halfway between Raharney and Killucan. It is reckoned that since the field was first purchased from the Irish Land Commission for what now seems a tiny sum of £500, the Raharney club has spent well in excess of a thousand times that amount transforming their park into a tremendous GAA facility.

The latest developments at Joristown Park, in addition to the excellent pitches, include a fine walking path around the perimeter of the pitch complex, and this 'Part of Joristown' scheme, for which they are selling metal plates, gives members and loyal supporters, including families, the chance to have their family name linked to the Joristown park, which has two fine full sizes pitches, and they have big plans to fully modernise their existing clubhouse and dressing rooms, which have the front walls adorned with photo plaques showing members of the Raharney Club's Westmeath Senior Championship winning side of 2014.

Incidentally, the special plates affixed to the fence around the park cost €70, €80 and €100, and orders can be arranged with Declan Weir. The annual membership for the new Walking Track is just €20, and this is new facility is proving attractive for many people, who want to enjoy the fresh air and open space in total safety whenever they want.

In April of this year, the President of the GAA, Aogán Ó Fearghail, was in Joristown to formally open the two new pitches, and was welcomed by Raharney Chairman, Billy Boyle, Secretary, Brendan Shaw, and the other club officials, with all GAA people in the area attending, and the

by Fr. Richard Matthews, PP and Fr. Frank Monks, OS Cam, from the Killucan Camillians, who have always been friends of the club.

HOW IT ALL BEGAN.....

The Joristown GAA Park had very interesting beginnings more than sixty years ago, and *Topic* spoke this week to two of the men, still hale and hearty, who were most closely involved at the time when the Raharney GAA club, a junior club at the time, first acquired the Joristown property.

Although most of today's generation would know little about the early years, Noel Weir was the man who played the key role in recognising the opportunity for Raharney club to obtain their own playing field in the early 1950s. At that time, Noel was a young shop boy in Raharney.

Noel told *Topic* that his memories were of seeing an advertisement in the paper about Joristown Demesne being divided by the Land Commission, and a line in the notice, saying that a GAA park would get priority if anyone applied.

"I decided to do something, as Club Secretary, so I applied on behalf of the club. Then I forgot all about it, and it was more than a year later when a man called in to me, and asked me where we wanted the GAA park. I couldn't even remember at first what he was talking about!

Then I realised who he was, and I contacted Seamus Brennan, the Principal of Raharney School, and the two of us went out with the Land Commission Inspector, to see what was being offered."

That's how Noel remembers the events of half a century or so ago, and he referred us to Seamus Brennan, retired Raharney Principal, for more detailed information.

The former Raharney headmaster wrote his own account of the origins of Joristown GAA park some

opments over the decades that followed its opening, and he kindly shared the details with *Topic* this week.

Mr. Brennan said that the Land Commission Inspector was Mr. Colleran from Mullingar, and after Noel Weir contacted him the day he called to the Raharney shop, the two of them went with Mr. Colleran up the Raharney-Corbettstown Road, to the avenue to what was the residence of late Col. Harvey Kelly. The Inspector pointed out a field to them, which was ideal in some ways. However, they felt it was too remote, and could have access difficulties, so they asked about an alternative. He then took them to what is now Joristown Park, and since it was beside the main road, and central, they decided to opt for it.

COST £380

"We were told we would have to pay £380 for it, and that the money could be paid in six monthly moieties, over two years. It seems nothing now, but it was a lot of money then," Seamus Brennan said.

"There were a lot of big mature trees growing on one side of the field, and we told the inspector they would have to sell the trees to get the money, but were informed we could not touch anything until the field was paid for."

"At that time, my wages as Principal were £6 a week," Mr. Brennan recalled, "so the money posed a problem for us, as credit was very tight. I approached my school manager, Fr. Farrelly, PP, and asked if he could loan money to us, and I said we would repay him when the trees were sold. He said he would consider it."

"I think he inspected the grounds and trees, as he came to me in the school the following day, and said he would advance the money, on condition he was made a trustee, and could hold on to the trust deeds until the money was repaid."

"Eddie King auctioned the trees, and we found were were able to repay Father Farrelly, and we actually had some money left over to start to develop

A view of the top clas pitch facilities now provided in Joristown GAA Park, with the walking track in the foreground.

Pictured outside the Raharney Clubhouse at Joristown Park this week were Seamus Brennan and Noel Weir.

in 1953 were Fr. Farrelly, Noel Weir, Seamus Brennan and Paddy McCabe. (In 1981, the then Trustees, Noel Weir, Seamus Brennan, the late Tommy Lynam and Ml. Flanagan were made full owners of Joristown Park in the Land Commission office in Dublin).

said. "I recall we decided to look for advice and help from leading GAA men to develop it, and we asked Paddy Bracken, a Leinster footballer, noted hurler Matty White, Matty Moore and Justin Graham - an agricultural instructor with Killucan Vocational School, and Matt Gartland, Chairman of Raharney Club at that time."

Mr. Brennan said rotovators were very scarce then, and "Noel and myself had to go to Rosenalis in Co. Laois to engage a man

and level the surface, which still had the remains of potato ridges. Justin Graham took on the job of seeding it, and I believe he brought out a group of boys from the school to pick the stones beforehand. I think this may have given rise to later claims that it was a parish park, but this was not true, as I have outlined," he said.

"The official opening was a very low-key affair, and Raharney team played Killyon, and as Killucan GAA Club had not yet been founded, a Killucan selection played The Downs. That original committee stayed on for some time," he said.

"Killucan Club was founded several years later, in 1957, and started using the park for training and matches. When Fr. Delany came as curate, being a strong GAA man and former County Board Chairman, we asked him for assistance. He built, with voluntary help, what is now the old dressing rooms and got a £90 GAA grant.

"In 1971, when the Camillian College closed, Fr. Monks offered a prefab free as a clubhouse, and Shay and Ber Murtagh brought it down and erected it, and it was in use for a good number of years, until it became dangerous, "

"Such were the events in the first two decades of Joristown," Seamus Brennan said.

[Image: Arc Studios]

"Raharney Centenary Year"

Welcome 1984, future what have you in store?
Will the village carve its name in Gaelic lore
What a joy it sure would be, GAA Centenary
Should the Deelside welcome Champions home once more

A Dinner Dance enjoyed by all, in the local Workman's Hall
Was a feat no club had ever done before
With the Wolfe Tones, funds did soar, money problems were now o'er
But would Deelside welcome Champions home once more

"Get your camán" was the cry "we must train in wet or dry"
"No man misses any training in the park"
With the Summer nearly o'er all our hopes began to soar
"We can do it" was the Chairman's fond remark.

Early rounds were now all past, five made it to the last
Hurling fever gripped the Blues as ne'er before
Ready bonfires, start the roar: get the Champagne from the store
And prepare to welcome Champions home once more

Minor, Sixteens gave their all and, in the end, alas did fall
Though the way they played their hearts out, made us proud
But the Juniors heights did soar, into Southern Gaels they tore
And Raharney cheered new Champions long and loud

Senior Final now in sight, Castletown Geoghegan at its might
Would Raharney under pressure wilt and crack
Smyth and Cleary at the back with the Captain Johnny Mac
Had to stop the Black and Ambers famed attack

Would the young lads conquer fear Mullen, Greville, Hickey, Weir
Would the Red and Lynch at centerfield hold sway
Would Shiels and Flanagan find their style, with Mullen, Donoghue, and Doyle
And help Greville pile the scores up on the day

Expectations were surpassed, the Blues all rose up to the task
In the greatest game Westmeath men can recall
Level five times in the game, in front, behind, in front again
Would the ref; oh, would the Ref, the full-time call

What a game Seán Greville played, vital scores he got or made
While young Doyle sent frees direct between the posts
When at last the whistle blew, after years we got our due
We had won the Cup Raharney wanted most.

Under Twenty Ones came of age, wrote another history page
As Clonkill they beat and won the Cup once more
Backroom boys had done their bit, Hon Sec Weir, and Chairman Smyth
They had steered the Club to heights not scaled before

When in future Deelside lore, they recall year '84
Top three hurling Cups to Deelside heroes bore
Light the bonfires, start the roar, get the Champagne from the store
Let us toast the Triple Champions, now once more

© Seamus Brennan

● A MAN AND HIS PIPE — Seamus Brennan, in typical pose with his trusty pipe.

Reaper & Binder in Rathrass

(Around 1931/1932) Pat Maguire, Jimmy Dargan (The Barret), Paddy Whelehan (The Fro), Vera Lynch (Grogan), Mynah Kilduff (Rooney), May Lynch (Sr. Marcellus).

Famous People with Connections to Raharney

'Giving Directions'

Standing on the roadside 35 years ago I met two Australian tourists a husband and wife, who were seeking directions as to where his wife's ancestors might have originated from, and where they might get some information. At the time I gave them whatever little help I could.

About a year later I got a letter thanking me for my help and telling me how successful they were in finding his wife ancestors'.

Before that day they had travelled extensively in Europe, attending Huguenot exhibitions in Amsterdam, Switzerland, France, and London. They were very determined to find her ancestors.

When I say a letter, it was 7 pages of A 4 extremely well handwritten and full of details about both their relatives that had left Ireland in 1800s, in totally different circumstances. This letter also piqued my interest in local history, in which I found a new interesting hobby.

I quote from some of this letter I received from Bruce and Leonie Casey summer 1987. With some additions from my own research.

"My wife Leonie's grandmother was born in Craddenstown, Raharney on the 17th June 1855 She was Evangeline Lahey one of eleven children born to Francis and Alicia Lahey, and baptised in St Etchen's Protestant Church, Killucan, who along with her parents and siblings emigrated to Australia in 1862. They were descendants of Francis La Haye who was born in the village of La-Hayeville in Lorraine about 200 miles from Paris. He was a Huguenot whose eldest son was killed on St Bartholomew's Day. He left France, in fact he fled to live in Westmeath. I believe 6-7,000 Huguenots came to live in Ireland and as he took his remaining eleven children with him there is no doubt many descendants of his are still living there. Huguenots were a highly skilled and industrious people both in the professions and trades and in all probability the majority who fled had some wealth, and those that were poor could not leave and were subjugated converted or slain. Such is the history of the poor in all countries and particularly in the name of religion. It is a sad reflection of the human race, that the main thing designed to bring people together and rejoice in, should be embraced to abuse others. Ireland certainly has had its fair share of this shameful treatment.

While my wife's Leonie's relatives from Raharney, Westmeath were protestant and relatively wealthy and travelled to Australia as a family unit with good facilities on the sailing ship the Bellissima Barque 431 ton from Liverpool in March arriving in Sydney on 28th July 1862 after nearly 4 months sailing. My ancestors from Cork were Catholic and poor. They travelled to Australia on convict ships. In 1828 and 1823 in atrocious conditions but survived. As you know several millions of Australians have Irish blood and a fair percentage of these have at least one convict in their ancestry. Both my Irish great grandparents were convicted in Ireland. My great grandfather Michael Casey was transported from Co Cork to Van Diemen's Land for 7 years penal servitude for steeling cattle. His wife Anne Hawthorne whom he met in Australia was transported for seven years for stealing a cloak. I have copies of their tickets of leave showing their transportation dates 1823 and 1828. They were sent to Bathurst.

Their Son Adam married and had seven children, one of whom James was my grandfather. Adam was murdered for his gold in the gold fields of "Kalgoorlie" western Australia. The gold rush brought many adventurous types "as well as villain's". Many Scots also come to Australia during the infamous clearance of the highlands by the Scottish Lairds. Many Welsh also from the grinding poverty of the coal mines and from the midlands of England and its industrial cities. My mother's mother came from Bradford whereas a child of seven she went to school for a half day and worked in a woollen mill as a "picker upper" for the other half.

In Ireland Leonie and I found there, a whispering sadness in the soft rain around the ruined remains of cottages that Irish people were evicted from and forced to leave long ago, particularly in the west coast of Ireland. The lingering melancholy surrounding the ruined castles that bring camera totting tourists. The view always appears different from where one is standing.
We were delighted with the courtesy and humour, of the people we met. I am sure you will be pleased to know we had a magnificent time in Ireland and the bond of heredity we have always felt has been strengthened by our brief contact with you and your lovely country which we will always remember with great affection.

Yours Sincerely
Bruce and Leonie Casey"

'The Laheys' Family Story'

Francis Lahey his wife Alicia and eleven children lived in Craddenstown as tenants of Lord Longford. They farmed a substantial farm of 108 acres until 1862. Frank Pender and his two sisters later lived on this farm for many years until their deaths in the 1960's. The farm was then purchased by the late Tommy Fleeson.

The Lahey's decided in 1862 as a family to emigrate to Australia. The situation in Ireland was not good at this time. Only a decade after the famine which had caused starvation, disease, death, and evictions, there was large scale emigration to England, Canada and America under terrible conditions with many deaths aboard those awful ships. The Lahey family would no doubt have some experience of

The Lahey Family - *Photograph courtesy of the John Oxley Library SLQ Neg 196712.*

the famine at the time growing up on a farm in Craddenstown close to where the dispensary for the Delvin Workhouse was situated where the starving, distressed, and poverty-stricken people went for help. Most of the children were of school going age at this time and would I'm sure have gone to the protestant school close by.

Conditions in Ireland at this time would not be a good place to bring up a large family of 11 children ranging in age from 4 to 18 years. "if there was another option."

Opportunity existed in Australia at the time for anyone with some capital, ambition, and hard work to be very successful.

Francis and Alicia Lahey would no doubt be aware of this. They lived through the famine and some of their children were born during this time. The decision to embark on this voyage would have taken a lot of thought, planning, courage, and money, all of which they obviously had. To leave Ireland for Australia at this time meant the likelihood of not seeing your family and friends in Ireland ever again. Their eleven children ranging in age, the eldest Margaret 18 years to the youngest David at 4 years of age and were all baptised in St Etchen's Protestant Church, Killucan. A local protestant school in Craddenstown was very close by and its presumed the children would have attended there and had many friends and neighbours and would be sad leaving.

The voyage they were embarking on would be a sort of an adventure for some of the children who would not fully understand the perils that lay ahead. However, the parents would certainly be aware of these. Their luggage and whatever they wished to take with them would be substantial.

In March 1862 the family left their home in Craddenstown on the start of their long voyage, first across to Liverpool by boat. They then boarded the Bellissima Barque 431 ton sailing ship in Liverpool as a family of 13 with only 1 other passenger William Armstrong who may have been a relative. They would have quite a lot of baggage, food would be provided for voyage by the captain in consultation with the cooks and the family, and water for such a long trip was also very important. I am sure there would be some commercial cargo on board to help pay for the voyage.

The ship had many crew members, 18 in total, including Captain John Whittle and 1st and 2nd mate 2 cooks, a carpenter, 2 Stewarts and the remaining 11 are able seamen as this is a 3-mast sailing ship.

Ireland was experiencing very high emigration around this time and certainly not in the relative luxury the Lahey Family were experiencing.

This voyage would no doubt be a daunting task considering the ages of the children. The great distance and the voyage was expected to take over 3 months. Sea sickness was going to be a difficult experience for everyone at the beginning, and for a while and during storms, which was the biggest worry for the parents, along with the worry of someone getting seriously ill on board, out on the ocean far away from any help. Also, with no wind becalming, another worry as this would lengthen the time
at sea.

David Lahey - *Photograph courtesy of the John Oxley Library SLQ Neg 196712.*

The voyage in fact took nearly 4 months and with eleven children on board their parent's courage in taking on such a voyage was amazing.

After many storms, frightening experiences, and sea sickness throughout the long voyage, the family landed in Sydney safe and well on board the Bellissima Barque on the 28th of July 1862. The family would have great exciting stories to tell their friends. Having been well looked after by a good Captain, two cooks, a large crew and with fair weather, having landed safely In Sydney they still had not reached their destination.

After a few more days sailing on a coaster boat, they arrived at their final destination Moreton Bay Brisbane.

They soon settled in Pimpama region and commenced farming arrowroot in 1870 and doing well. Two members of the Family John and Alicia returned to Ireland later. John worked with an uncle, for a period but returned to Australia. Alicia married someone named Strong and lived in Co Cavan and had 4 children. She died during the first world war.

Francis soon expanded the operations and purchased a sugar mill at Tygum for his sons and constructed a timber sawmill in 1875.

As a family they worked hard together and were innovative, and very successful, and by the turn of the twentieth century it was the largest wood milling business in Queenstown and the largest softwood milling business in Australia.

David who married Jane Jemima Walmsley in 1881 and had a large family of twelve children that included the artist FRANCES VIDA LAHEY, and Romeo Lahey the famous conservationist who was mostly responsible for creation of Lamington National Park. He was the founding President of the National Parks Association of Queensland.

The site of the Lahey sawmill is now a heritage site on the Queensland Heritage Register.

© *Shay Callaghan*

Francis Vida Lahey M.B.E.

One of Australia's most famous artist Francis Vida Lahey M.B.E. born 26th August 1882, died August 1968. Travelled widely and studied in Brisbane, London, Paris and Italy. She was awarded the society of N.S.W. medal in 1945. The coronation medal in 1953 and in 1958 awarded an M.B.E. in recognition of her contribution to art in Australia. Her father David Lahey emigrated from Craddenstown , Raharney in 1862 with his parents Francis and Alicia Lahey and 10 siblings.

Francis Lahey - Photograph courtesy of https://learning. qagoma.qld.gov.au/artworks/ monday-morning/

The Academic

Westmeath, with a population of just under 100,000 people, has a disproportionate claim on Irish musical talent when compared to neighbouring counties. Raharney, with a population of under 500 people, can claim two such musicians, the Murtagh brothers of Joristown. Stephen and Matt Murtagh grew up on Rodneys Hill and attended St Marys national school before attending St Josephs Secondary school in Rochfortbridge where they met local boy Dean Gavin and Craig Fitzgerald of Rathwire (originally Dublin). This four piece would soon become known as The Academic. Both brothers accredit their musical taste to their upbringing both at home and in school. Matts first public guitar performance was for his friends in St Marys, and Stephen remembers hearing The Beatles and ABBA for the first time in the classroom, via his national school teachers.

Playing at band nights in Mullingar pubs and weekend festivals in the town centre, the young musicians of The Academic were able to test their earliest work on the critics of the lake county. YouTube videos of the bands acoustic performances were shared nationwide, often featuring a local Raharney garden or shed where they would practice together. Going from strength to strength, they released an EP named 'Loose Friends' in 2015 and in the same year sold out Dublin's Vicar Street, playing hit sings such as Different and Northern Boy to a 1500 strong crowd. As cyclone storm Eleanor swept Ireland in January 2018, The Academic independently released their debut album 'Tales From the Backseat' to a frenzy of attention, entering the Official Irish Albums Chart at number one. The album was nominated for Album of the Year at the Choice Music Prize in January 2019.

Following the release of their album, the band toured extensively across Europe and North America, playing to a variety of fans in sold out venues around the globe. The commercial success and critical acclaim of The Academic could be attributed to their dedication and work ethic, as all their releases had been independent thus far. The attention garnered by a band working under their own steam had caught the eyes and ears of major record labels, and in early 2020 ,The Academic signed a worldwide record deal with Capitol Records; the home of Paul McCartney, Sam Smith and fellow Westmeath native Niall Horan. Since then, they've released two more EPs (2020's Acting My Age and 2021's Community Spirit). Having shared the stage with The Strokes, Noel Gallagher and The Killers, as well as a once in a lifetime opportunity opening for The Rolling Stones in Croke Park, the band has grown to extents unseen in local battle of the band competitions and school shows. At the time of writing, the band hold their audience in suspense ahead of the release of their second full length album, expected in 2023.

Raharney Reeling in the Years

RAHARNEY BAND: Members of the youthful Raharney

When the Council purchased Belvedere...

Raharney, Nuachleas winners, left to right, Nicola Morley, Lily Connaughton (coach), Brian Connaughton, Pamela Greville, Jordon Greville, Philip Weir, Noleen Lynam (coach), Damien Murtagh and Louise McManus in front.

(1) Brian Connaughton, Dessie McKeogh, Jimmy Weir, Chrissie Goonery *(2)* Paddy Cunningham, Mick Dargan *(3)* Brendan Sheils, Jimmy Flynn *(4)* Teresa Lynch, Joe Lynch, Jimmy & Paddy Nolan *(5)* Garty's Shop *(6)* Kevin Gooney, Margaret Farrelly, Lillie Connaughton, Tommy McManus.

Raharney Reeling in the Years

(1) Kathleen & Tommy O'Reilly *(2)* Ned Dargan (2nd from left) *(3)* Leo Dargan *(4)* Leo Dargan (on combine) *(5)* Ned Lynch, Craddenstown 1955 *(6)* William Dargan *(7)* Cusack Park 1965 *(8)* Kathy McKeogh *(9)* William Dargan breaking in a young horse *(10)* Harvesting turf in Bellview.